TIFFANY PARTIES

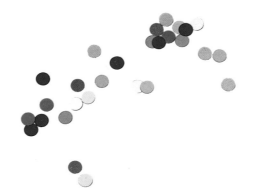

TIFFANY PARTIES

JOHN LORING

PREFACE BY AILEEN MEHLE
FOREWORD BY JOHN LORING
INTRODUCTION BY JANE LANE

Doubleday

NEW YORK LONDON TORONTO SYDNEY AUCKLAND

Also by John Loring
  The Tiffany Wedding
  Tiffany's 150 Years
  Tiffany Taste
  The New Tiffany Table Settings
    (with Henry B. Platt)

Designed by Jean-Claude Suarès
Assisted by Gates Studio

Acknowledgments
Tiffany & Co. gratefully acknowledges the
exceptional contributions of Yone Akiyama,
Tiffany's Associate Director of Design, for her
role as director of photography; Mr. William
R. Chaney, Chairman of the Board of
Tiffany's, for his generous support of so many
of the charity galas illustrated in this book;
Nancy Holmes for her invaluable guidance
through the labyrinths of American society;
Rita Eckartt for her life-saving assistance as
travel and traffic director; Crary Pullen for
her diligence in research.

Published by Doubleday
a division of Bantam Doubleday Dell
Publishing Group, Inc.
666 Fifth Avenue, New York, New York
10103

Doubleday *and the portrayal of an anchor*
with a dolphin are trademarks of Doubleday,
a division of Bantam Doubleday Dell
Publishing Group, Inc.

Library of Congress Cataloging-in-
Publication Data

Loring, John,
    Tiffany parties / John Loring : preface
by Aileen Mehle: foreword by John Loring:
introduction by Jane Lane,—1st ed.
        p.   cm.
    1. United States—Social life and
customs—1971–   2. Entertaining—United
States—History—20th century.   I. Title.
E169.04.L67   1989
973—dc20   89-7730   CIP

ISBN 0-385-26352-X
Copyright © 1989 by Tiffany & Co.
All Rights Reserved
Printed in Italy
November 1989
First Edition
NIL

Contents

Preface by Aileen Mehle

9

Foreword by John Loring

18

Introduction by Jane Lane

23

New York Public Library Ten Treasures Dinner

28

Irving Berlin's 100th Birthday, New York

34

The New York Philharmonic Ball

38

An Evening with Calvin Klein to Benefit the Ellington
Fund, Washington, D.C.

42

The Nelson A. Rockefeller Public Service Award
Dinner, New York

46

Mrs. John Kluge's Birthday Party, New York

50

The Opening of the New York Central Park Zoo

54

Ambassador and Countess Wachtmeister's Dinner,
Washington, D.C.

56

Mrs. Virginia S. Milner's Hawaiian Luau Honoring
Mr. and Mrs. Walter Annenberg, Beverly Hills

60

Mrs. Lawrence Copley Thaw's Dinner in Honor of
Mrs. Guilford Dudley, Jr., New York

64

Mr. and Mrs. Milton Petrie's Fourth of July Party,
Southampton

68

Walter Gubelmann's Eightieth Birthday Party,
Newport

72

The Tiffany Feather Ball, New York

74

Contents

The Swan Ball, Nashville
78

The Southampton Hospital Ball
82

Blair House Tea Reception, Washington, D.C.
86

Lintas Worldwide Reception, New York
92

Green Animals Children's Picnic, Newport
98

The Parrish Art Museum Dance, Southampton
100

Bernstein at Seventy, Boston
104

Snowmass Picnic, Colorado
108

Cocktails Aboard the *Trump Princess,* New York
114

The Atlanta Symphony Ball
118

Geoffrey Beene/The First Twenty-Five Years,
New York
122

The Lyric Opera of Chicago Ball
126

Alice in Wonderland or A Kid Again, Greenwich
130

The Splendour in St. Petersburg Ball, Old Westbury
134

Hispanic Designers' Luncheon for Paloma Picasso,
Washington, D.C.
140

The Union Station Gala, Washington, D.C.
144

Paige Rense's New York Winter Antiques Show
Dinner
152

The Tiffany Wedding Dinner, New York
154

Contents

The Chicago Opera Theater Gala
158

The Brooklyn Academy of Music's Gala of Stars
162

The 1988 Royal Chase Committee Luncheon,
Nashville
166

The Stop Cancer Gala at the Winter Garden,
New York
170

The Coconuts' New Year's Eve, Palm Beach
174

The Literary Lions Dinner, New York
176

The Reagans' Final State Dinner, Washington, D.C.
178

State Department Dinner in Honor of Secretary of
State and Mrs. George P. Shultz, Washington, D.C.
184

Mr. and Mrs. David Paul's Six Chefs Dinner,
La Gorce Island
188

The Metropolitan Museum of Art's Costume Institute
Gala, New York
192

Mrs. Albert Lasker's Annual December Dinner,
New York
194

Katharine Johnson's Dinner, New York
198

Spirit of the City Award Dinner, New York
200

The Baron and Baroness di Portanova's Christmas
Party, Houston
202

Photography Credits
208

Preface

I've been to some marvelous parties, really I have, man and boy. It's what I do best—almost every night. I've also been to some awful duds where the hostess could well have been banished from the kingdom for the crimes of bad timing, bad lighting, bad food and ghastly guests. But I wouldn't dream of boring you with all that. So, let's drop rose petals into our Tiffany crystal finger bowls and wash our hands of *them*, shall we?

All marvelous parties share three things in common—imagination, a desire to dazzle and delight, and a transcendent guest list.

I've been to glamorous gatherings in Palm Beach on board Aristotle Onassis's floating palace *Christina* when free-spirited Ari never stopped recounting his Rabelaisian exploits and Jackie, cool in white silk pants and a ruby or two (big ones) charmed lovers of eighteenth-century furniture Jayne and Charles Wrightsman while the famous Mexican society beauty Gloria Guinness wigwagged her kitten hips to the music. I would love to tell you the precious mosaic swimming pool on deck was filled with champagne, but it wasn't. Everyone else was.

I've been to fabled parties in Europe, grand galas guaranteed to take your breath away—months, sometimes years, in the planning. The most lavish were invariably costume balls with a fancy theme. (The French are so good at *fantaisie, n'est-ce pas*? Set in a magnificent château in the countryside or a ravishing *hôtel particulier* in Paris, these fêtes drew the most dazzling guests—beautiful seductive women in extravagant *maquillage*, rich and powerful men, some of them even distinguished. All were beautifully bedecked, bejeweled, coiffed, perfumed and masked to the nines. One gasped at the splendor, breathed in the aroma of a hundred thousand flowers and thanked heaven, and the hosts, for the invitation.

Can I ever forget the Baron and Baroness Guy de Rothschild's glittering Proust Ball at Ferrières, their spectacular château outside Paris? *Pas du tout.* Marcel himself would have envied the cast and the setting. Here are the Duke and Duchess of Windsor, she blazing with jewels, both spreading their wings in opposite directions. There, limpid-eyed, is Hélène Rochas, the Paris perfume queen, cameos and camellias at her throat, being immortalized by Cecil Beaton, the "court photographer" for the night, attired in an artist's smock and velvet beret lest anyone forget he is a personage. Stunning Marisa Berenson, then the inamorata of Rothschild son and heir David, has got herself up as the mad Marchesa Casati, who loved leading a leopard on a leash—but with wild plumes in her hair and an outrageously long cigarette

(Opposite) *Miss Hedwig Reicher, dressed as Cleopatra, admires Ruth St. Denis dancing at Louis Comfort Tiffany's Egyptian fête held in Tiffany Studios, New York, on February 4, 1913. The fête, said the* New York Times *three days later, "eclipsed any fancy dress function ever presented in New York."*

Guests included Mrs. John D. Rockefeller, Jr., as Minerva; Mr. Rockefeller as a Persian; Mrs. Edward S. Harkness as Potiphar's wife; Mr. Harkness as an Egyptian; Mrs. Cleveland Dodge; Miss Dorothy Roosevelt as a Persian; Mr. and Mrs. George W. Seligman as a Greek water-bearer and an Arabian sheik; Hiram Bingham as an Arabian; and others too costumed to mention.

(Above) *Louis Comfort Tiffany admires Miss Hedwig Reicher's Cleopatra costume at his "Fête Egyptian."*

(Right) *Guests at Louis Comfort Tiffany's Egyptian fête included his daughter-in-law Mrs. Charles L. Tiffany, Jr., as Cleopatra with scarab wings; and* (opposite, from top to bottom) *Hiram Bingham as an Arabian and Frieda Tiffany Mitchell Bingham as an Egyptian; "L.C.T.'s" granddaughters Misses Mary, Julia and Dorothy Tiffany, all as Egyptians; and Mrs. John A. Hartwell as an Egyptian queen crowned with bird-of-paradise feathers.*

holder, Marisa is more madwoman of Chaillot. Elizabeth Taylor, a diamond necklace attached to her forehead, the famous pouter pigeon breast erupting from a nest of lace, can't keep her hands off Richard Burton—and vice versa. The hostess, Marie-Hélène de Rothschild, the unquestioned empress of Paris society—she has only to snap her fingers and the sybarites (do I mean sycophants?) swarm—is clad in a disarmingly simple white satin frock worth a fortune and wears matching marquise diamonds on her pinkies worth a Rothschild's ransom.

The tables are covered in pleated mauve chiffon adorned with mountains of purple orchids, the exotic bloom that was Odette Swann's favorite flower. I would love to tell you we ate lotus for dinner, but my remembrance of things past tells me it was merely lobster—or perhaps roast quail.

And oh, the brilliant Oriental Ball given by the elegant Baron Alexis de Redé at the Hôtel Lambert, one of the most glorious private houses in Paris, which he and the Guy de Rothschilds call home! Two enormous white elephants (ersatz), richly caparisoned and bearing mahouts in golden howdahs, flank the cobbled courtyard. Bedazzled guests climb the grand staircase guarded by giant Nubian slaves carrying great torches to find Alexis waiting at the top. His face enameled chalk-white, he is dressed as a Russian prince, all in black from his wide fur hat to his narrow black boots on feet too slender to be true.

Everyone is there in magical Orientalia including an alluring Brigitte Bardot at the peak of her sex-kitten beauty, covered in two inches of golden gauze, moving sinuously through Alexis's sumptuous apartments which Jean-

François Daigre, who always does the Rothschilds' fêtes, has been called in to decorate in his incomparable opulent style. Even Prince Johannes von Thurn und Taxis, whose German castle is bigger than Buckingham Palace, is impressed to his eyebrows which have been painted a grotesque black for the evening to go with his grotesquely painted red mouth.

The pleasure-bent, life-loving Bolivian tin king Antenor Patino, a man of exquisite taste, was a matchless host. When he and his Spanish-born wife Beatriz gave a great ball at their far-flung finca in Portugal, a mini-Versailles with gardens, waterfalls and fountains to burn, it set a dazzling standard by which all truly grand parties are measured. The privileged guests came from miles around and across the sea, and once again Jean-François Daigre, in partnership with the international interior designer Valerian Rybar, was asked to spin a web. Using Portugal's colors, red and green, they transformed the terraces of this most beautiful of houses into green-turreted Manueline pavilions elaborately illuminated by twenty thousand huge hurricane lamps. Enormous coral chandeliers swung overhead. These and the red-and-green-print satin tablecloths and napkins bearing the Patino monogram and crest, the crystal and the silver table settings were all especially made for the party. The forty-foot-long buffet tables, built in tiers, were laden with towering, fanciful arrangements, still lifes come to life, some of them six feet tall, of gigantic lobsters surrounded by gorgeous flowers, fruits and vegetables, all interspersed with priceless silver objects from the Patinos' extraordinary collection. All of us not already swooning almost fainted dead away at the sight of Eugenie Niarchos, the wife of shipping Midas Stavros Niarchos, floating by with the Niarchos diamond, one hundred and eight flawless carats, reposing on her bosom. When the cream of international society tired of dancing in the terraced nightclub, they threw themselves on hundreds of silken cushions, the women spreading the skirts of their killer ball gowns from Saint Laurent, Valentino and Dior around them.

Most of us lolling on Patino pillows were still reeling from the glories of another Portuguese extravaganza given two nights earlier at their fantastic finca nearby by São Schlumberger and her husband Pierre, the oil well equipment tycoon. It was a gala so stunning that several social desperadoes employed cunning ruses to elicit invitations, some even flying into Lisbon on spec. They were no match for Mme. Schlumberger, who, in jewels shimmering like the *azulêjos* in her picturesque grotto, was said to have turned a movie star away at the door.

For the wondrous costume ball given at their beautiful house on the sea in Greece, the acclaimed hosts Rosemarie and Jean Pierre Marcie-Rivière, who have given famous parties on several continents, chose an Orientalist theme suggested by their extensive collection of Orientalist paintings throughout the house. The terraces looking out on the water were laid with Persian rugs, and guests reclined on the floor against huge bolsters and leaned against richly colored cushions of velvet, silk and satin as they dined at low tables, stirring the balmy night air with the gold and silver fans that were presents from the hosts. *La belle* Rosemarie, dressed as the Sultan's favorite, in a jeweled bra and more or less see-through harem pants, had cooks flown from Morocco just to make the couscous. Sixteen splendid yachts, including Henry Ford's and the Harding Lawrences', steamed in for the party and stayed for three days. As a change from the ladies running around in practically nothing—Francesca Thyssen danced in one, not seven veils—the Duchess of Bedford was in her own private purdah, completely covered from head to toe in a yellow tent with only tiny slits for her eyes. The Duke of Bedford just shook his head and rolled his eyes a lot.

Whatever the luxury of their revels, one must never conclude that the Europeans have a corner on the marvelous party market. They just got started before the Americans did and now, with governments changing, the grand gala-givers have run out of steam and, in a few cases, money. Many of their gandiose establishments have been sold, those stone-and-marble monuments the Vanderbilts and Astors copied, now too mammoth for a single family to maintain. Marie-Hélène de Rothschild's balls are now given at, say, the Louvre, and for charity. As for the British, the galas held at such magnificent stately homes as Sutton Place, Broadlands and Blenheim Palace, in the presence of the Prince and Princess of Wales, are either for charity or to repair acres of leaking roofs.

Enter the Americans. Enter Truman Capote, that mischievous elf, whose Black and White Masked Ball at the Plaza given for Katharine Graham, the owner of the *Washington Post*, entered the annals of legendary parties, spectacularly publicized.

The big thing Truman had going for him was an incredible guest list made up of five hundred and forty undeniable stars of society, government, the arts, and the nobility, plus a passel of multimillionaires and their decorative wives. The security was so dense as to be obscene.

Truman, who planned the party six months ahead of time, wanted a masked ball for the fun and the mystery of it. The gentlemen wore dinner jackets and black dominoes. The ladies wore black and white ball gowns and fantasy masks, jeweled and feathered. Even Peter Duchin and the members of his orchestra were in masks. Truman thought the ornate white-and-gold ballroom, which he considered the only beautiful one left in the United States, could take care of itself, so he kept the décor simple—crimson tablecloths, tall white tapers, tons of smilax, that was just about it. But because of the richness and renown of the men and the radiance of the beautiful women the room fairly shimmered. Mrs. Nicholas Longworth, Teddy Roosevelt's tart-tongued daughter Alice, arrived, predictably, in a mask she bought at the dime store. Oscar de la Renta and Françoise de Langlade each wore an extraordinary cat mask with silken whiskers, his an inky black, hers a pristine white; Billy Baldwin, dean of interior designers, wore a unicorn's head. Rose Kennedy was there and Lynda Bird Johnson, Claudette Colbert, Lauren Bacall, Tallulah Bankhead, Kitty and Gilbert Miller, Candice Bergen, Gloria Guinness, Lee Radziwill, Margaret Truman, Phyllis and Bennett Cerf, Cecil Beaton, Evangeline and David Bruce, Gloria Vanderbilt; Marella and Gianni Agnelli, S. N. Behrman, Charlotte Ford, Pat and Bill Buckley, Drue and Jack Heinz and others equally coruscant. All guests were announced as they entered the ballroom, and it was the first time I had ever seen the enchanting, young Penelope Tree. Dressed as a wood nymph, she looked more like a sylvan creature wafted in on a zephyr than a fine lady at the ball of the decade.

Truman had his day—and his magic night—but to my mind, *the* party of American parties was the joyous extravaganza given by Drue Heinz to celebrate her husband Henry J. (Jack) Heinz II's seventy-fifth birthday. Drue had polished her act earlier on at her party for Jack's fifty-seventh (fifty-seven for Heinz's 57 varieties of food products) birthday at their country house in Bedford, New York, a sensational affair complete with city slickers and the surrounding gentry all done up in Gay Nineties attire, but that was only a warm-up for what was to come eighteen years later.

The Heinzes' superb city house on Sutton Place backs onto a glorious block-long garden with beautiful old trees and great sweeping lawns, a *tapis vert* stretching down to the East River. Peggy Mulholland, the talented young party decorator, was called in to work with Drue and what they wrought will be spoken of for years to come by the four hundred guests and the thousands that heard about it. Boar Park, the little square at Sutton Place directly in front of the Heinz house, was transformed into a miniature carnival *cum* street fair. There were jugglers and clowns, mimes and mountebanks and an oyster shucker in hip boots displaying his wares at a bar banked in ice and seaweed. A juggler dressed like a tomato teetered on a tightrope. A huge ketchup bottle, really a remote-control robot, greeted the guests. A Dixieland band flown from New Orleans tooted and twanged. Guests, again dressed

The many dazzling balls in the Versailles Room of New York's St. Regis Hotel that Henry B. Platt, ex-Tiffany president and great-grandson of Louis Comfort Tiffany, gave in the sixties and seventies were, as Jane Lane noted in W, *celebrated "not because of the arrangements which [were] quite simple, but the guests themselves. Flocks of beautiful young girls, handsome swains, titled nobility, ladies gleaming with jewels, refined gentlemen and the just plain rich."*

(Opposite, top) *Henry B. Platt poses with Aileen Mehle, "Suzy," at the last Platt ball, in December of 1980. It was, she wrote, "just too much—too many beauties, too many fabulous dresses, too much shimmering flesh, too many men with their heads spinning in all directions.*

"Show me Harry Platt at his party," she added, "and I'll show you a sultan in a seraglio."

in Gay Nineties costumes in honor of Jack, who was born shortly after the turn of the century, had their pictures taken on a bicycle built for two.

Under three connecting tents in the garden, dinner tables, covered with burlap and centered with silver colanders spilling over the miniature fruits, vegetables and a magnum of champagne, were set up. Hollowed-out artichokes held votive candles, and placecards sat on fat upside-down mushrooms. Luxuriant hydroponic tomato plants grew up the tent poles and ran riot over the latticework along the sides of the tents. Waiters with handlebar mustaches, wearing straw boaters and striped vests, served forty birthday cakes surrounded by spun sugar and sparklers on silver platters, one to each table. On the dance floor, Floradora girls and high-class ladies in feather boas and jeweled headbands tripped to the music of Peter Duchin and his orchestra. And that was only on the inside.

Outside, in the beautiful bucolic setting, sheep grazed on the lawns, pretty Gibson girls floated on flower-festooned swings and owls hooted from the trees. At the bottom of the garden, the iron railings along the river reaching from 57th to 58th Street were hung with great garlands of luscious fruits and vegetables. At the witching hour there was a spectacular display of fireworks bursting from a barge on the river, ending with the message, "JUMPING JACK, STILL IN A PICKLE AT 75," spelled out in flashing pyrotechnics. What a night! In the rockets' red glare could be seen the Henry Kissingers, the William F. Buckleys, the Henry Fords, Lady Keith, the Irving Lazars, Mike Nichols, Renata Adler, Irene Selznick and others too razzled and dazzled to mention.

How to describe all these divine divertissements without writing a book? Mary and Harding Lawrence's parties at their romantic villa La Fiorentina at Saint-Jean-Cap-Ferrat in the South of France, one of the most incredibly beautiful houses in that part of the world, with lush gardens to the sea, a topiary dream. The Lawrences' food and music are the best there is, and I saw Princess Grace of Monaco having the time of her life there.

Or the coruscant villa-warming of La Léopolda, the fantastic Ogden Codman-designed residence in Villefranche where the international banker Edmond Safra and his decorative wife Lily celebrated with a grand ball the miracle Renzo Mongiardino, the famed interior designer, had wrought with the greatest furniture and objects taste and money can buy.

Or Princess Margaret and Lord Snowdon's intimately glamorous party for fashion legend Diana Vreeland at their Grace and Favour flat in Kensington Palace. Elizabeth Taylor and a flirtatious Richard Burton—he flirted with everyone but Elizabeth—stayed late and so did the best ambassadors and ambassadresses and an absolute exaltation of pretty young things.

Or Ivana and Donald Trump's terrific house parties at Mar-a-Lago, their gorgeous Palm Beach estate stretching from sea to lake. It once was the winter home of the late heiress and hostess Marjorie Merriweather Post, who, luckily for the Trumps, left behind mountains of her crystal and vermeil, and golden épergnes as big as the doodads at Buckingham Palace.

Or state dinners at the White House honoring the most powerful people on earth, the Lincoln Dining Room aglow with roses and the Reagan china gleaming.

Gold stars, a whole skyful, to the Baron and Baroness Enrico di Portanova for their movie star-glamorous parties thrown nonstop at their multiterraced, multilevel pleasure dome, Arabesque, in Acapulco—one of the most dramatic houses in the world, with a dozen life-size white plaster camels ruminating on the terrace.

And the not-to-be-forgotten harvest ball at Patricia and second-richest-man-in-the-country John Kluge's immense manor house, Albemarle, set in the middle of thousands of rolling acres of Virginia land. There were haystacks and blooded bulls in the stables and elegant carriages pulled by elegant horses and any number of black and white swans floating on the Kluges' myriad man-made lakes and an awful lot of pumpkins and pheasants *en plumage*. Party planner Clive David organized the festivities that lasted for three days.

In New York, there are marvelous Manhattan parties—at the Metropolitan Museum with Pat Buckley at the helm of the Costume Institute's annual fling—at the Museum of Modern Art and the National Academy of Design—at the New York Public Library—at the Metropolitan Opera where socialite Cecile Zilkha organizes enchanted evenings onstage and off. The wonder of these galas is that they seem effortless. In reality, they call for all the imagination and energies a host and hostess can bring to bear.

Mrs. Guilford Dudley, Jr., dances at the 1980 Platt Ball.

Is it all right to save the best for the last? Perhaps I'm prejudiced, but to me the Gold and Silver Bal Masqué, "In Celebration of Suzy," in the Plaza's Grand Ballroom was everything a perfectly flawless, flawlessly perfect party should be. (Oh well, maybe the Suprême de Volaille aux Chanterelles à Blanc en Cocotte was a tiny bit dry—but what the hell!) One of the reasons it was such a tremendously exciting night was because it was different from anything they'd had around here for years. Europeans adore tableaux and costumes and masked balls, but when you mention wearing something other than a long dress and a black tie to a fête, even some of the most sophisticated Americans go all nervous and insecure and apprehensive. However—once you shove the bit in their teeth, there is no holding them back.

For that one night only, the Plaza opened up the Palm Court entrance to the Terrace Room so that the four hundred guests, the ladies dressed in gold and silver, wearing the most ornately feathered and sequinned gold and silver fantasy masks, and the gentlemen, masked as well (Douglas Fairbanks, Jr., wore a gold horse's head; Mario Buatta wore a gold lampshade) were able to sweep straight through to cocktails in the Terrace Room without having to climb the stairs to the usual side entrance.

In the Palm Court, the famous photographer Norman Parkinson had set up a studio where the bedecked guests were photographed for posterity— and for *Town & Country*. But the excitement peaked in the Terrace Room where, floating in champagne, surrounded by the most wonderful plants and flowers and looking absolutely dewy in the perfect lighting, the four hundred swooned and screamed over the beauty of the masks and tried to guess who was behind them. It was such fun that when the time came to go in to dinner, they almost had to be forcibly ejected.

But oh, the sight that met their eyes when they entered the Grand Ballroom! Such gasps, such cries of "Did you ever see anything more beautiful?" John Funt, Tiffany & Co.'s design genius, had transformed the room into the glittering winter conservatory of a Russian crystal palace, one a czarina wouldn't have sneezed at. In the center of each of the tables towered a giant crystal palm tree, its fronds hung with one thousand Czechoslovakian crystal prisms arching gracefully over the table. The enormous trunks of the trees were swathed in gold lamé over which climbed clusters of pale peach and yellow roses. Grapevines painted gold entwined the trunks and twirled upward, ending in great sprays of white orchids bursting from the tops of the shimmering trees. All was bathed in peach light.

Yellow rambler roses were arranged in little nosegays at the base of the trees and votive candles were nestled in the surrounding moss. The tables were covered in silver lamé to the floor with overlay cloths of gold lamé. The napkins were pale peach linen, and the downy cushions of the chairs were a darker shade of peach. There were silver service plates and silver-and-crystal swans holding sea salt and freshly ground pepper. The favors were silver pens from Tiffany. The effect? Nothing short of breathtaking!

This was the big surprise of the evening! Small tables covered in gold and silver were set up in each of the white orchid-banked boxes or loges surrounding the ballroom and there—lolling on the balustrades and balconies, sipping champagne, dancing the tango on the tabletops, flirting and peering out at the guests through opera glasses—were dozens of devastatingly beautiful, lifelike mannequins from Saks Fifth Avenue, all masked, all jeweled, all dressed to the nines, some of them wearing dresses owned by the ladies of the committee. One abandoned Lady Godiva-type hussy was lying on her back, completely naked unless you counted her long yellow hair. They flaunted elaborate cigarette holders and long white gloves and they all stared at the guests who stared back at them, unable to believe they weren't real. The exception was an exotic *ersatz* Comtesse de Ribes, a stunning replica of the real thing, the French fashion plate Jacqueline de Ribes, who sat in her loge surrounded by her court, an entourage of *soigné* and suave gentlemen (synthetic, to be sure) who had eyes only for her, forget about the action in the ballroom. Meanwhile, the real thing, the *true* Comtesse, who arrived at the ball in a diamond dog collar and dangling diamond earrings, laughed her little *à la Française* laugh as she regarded her model mirror image. What panache!

At the 1980 Platt Ball, Comtesse Jacqueline de Ribes chats with Carolina Herrera while Renaldo Herrera and Mrs. Oscar Wyatt look on.

Not content with banking the boxes with all the white orchids he could muster, John Funt had placed tall weeping beeches sparkling with twinkle-lights and set in gold tubs crammed with peach roses between each loge. The idea was that everywhere the eye fell there was beauty—and there was.

Vince Giordano and the Nighthawks played for the dancing, and record tycoon Ahmet Ertegun provided a hot—and loud—Latin orchestra to spell them.

Even the invitations were a collector's item. Complete with a silken tassel and a little crystal ball, they were designed by the celebrated illustrator Joe Eula, who painted on the cover an alluring masked beauty wearing sexy earrings and a tulle headdress.

The ball, which netted $460,000 for the Society of Memorial Sloan-Kettering—I wanted it that way—was the fabulous result of monumental work by Pat Buckley, Marilyn Evins and Jane Dudley and the generosity of a score of patrons and benefactors. In the crowd were such worthies as Princess Margaret, Drue Heinz, Nancy Kissinger, Princess Yasmin Aga Khan, Linda Robinson, Anne Bass, Mica Ertegun, Consuelo Crespi, Ann Getty, Betsy Bloomingdale, Patty Cisneros, Fernanda Niven; Carolina Herrera, Lyn Revson, Mercedes Kellogg, Judy Peabody, Estée Lauder, Evelyn Lauder, Chessy Rayner, Mary Wells Lawrence, Anne Slater, Denise Hale, Nan Kempner, Josie Wilson, their husbands and escorts and others too scintillating to mention.

But enough of all that. I must leave you now. I'm late, I'm late for a very important date. You see, I'm off to a—marvelous party! Maybe I'll see you there!

Aileen Mehle

Foreword

(Above, top) *Guests at the July 13, 1957, Tiffany Ball dance in the Gold Room of Newport's Marble House.*

(Bottom) *A Tiffany vermeil service decorates the 34-foot-long table in the mansion's pink marble dining room where Tiffany's 1,200 guests enjoyed a midnight supper of ham, turkey, eggs and sausage.*

(Opposite) *Mrs. John R. Drexel III greets her recently married friends, Senator and Mrs. John F. Kennedy, in the entrance hall of Marble House.*

Call them fêtes; call them galas or balls or dinner dances; or just call them what they are, big parties. However labeled and however observed—whether from the viewpoint of sociology or design, economics or politics, fashion or philanthropy—parties offer a rich-textured and revealing spectacle of their times. At them, the great of the world parade, show their colors and amuse their fellowmen, while social observers chronicle their antics.

Much has been told of the legendary European forerunners of today's big parties: In Paris, Paul Poiret's "1,001 Nights" costume fête of 1911; the Pecci-Blunts' White Ball designed by Man Ray in 1930; the extravagant evenings of Count Étienne de Beaumont so notably parodied by Raymond Radiguet in *Le Bal du Comte d'Orgel;* and Carlos de Beistegui's fabled Venetian Ball on September 3, 1951, in the Palazzo Labia. This last celebration has been so overpublicized as "the party of the century" that memory and reality seem at odds. The glamour of the twenties and thirties, six years after World War II, had simply not been rediscovered. But maybe you had, as they say, to be there.

America too had its share of legendary forerunners of today's big parties, with their own Yankee flavor: the Vanderbilts' fêtes in their Ritz Hotel-like "cottages" in Newport before World War I; Louis Comfort Tiffany's Egyptian Ball of February 1913; Caroline Astor's evenings for New York's Four Hundred at her Fifth Avenue and 65th Street mansion, and more recently Truman Capote's Black and White Masked Ball for 540 of the select at New York's Plaza Hotel in the autumn of 1966. It was the Capote ball which heralded a new era of parties infused with that insatiable American appetite for entertainment, that quality George Gershwin called "our incomparable national pep," "our metropolitan madness."

In the 1980s the American party has matured and come into its own with razzle-dazzle glamour that makes the poor old black-and-white photos of de Beistegui's Venetian Ball look downright dull. Today's great American social/charitable events are a remarkable, supremely photogenic phenomenon of our age.

Big American parties, however, are only partially covered by the press. The gossip columnists Aileen Mehle, William Norwich, Liz Smith and George Christie describe them. "Suzy" calls roll. The fashion press perfunctorily illustrates the socially celebrated and what they wear, graded with stars or "ins" or "outs" or "F.V.s" (for "Fashion Victims")—but the wondrous and extravagant décors go unrecorded.

Tiffany Parties provides a unique social document of the times, the end of the Reagan era and the settings of its celebratory mood, whose buoyant delight in the lavishly, splendidly ephemeral has not been seen since the great balls of eighteenth-century Europe.

Everyone with the slightest interest in American society is familiar with photographs of our grandest social ladies as they arrive at parties: Mrs. William F. Buckley in a Bill Blass, Mrs. Saul Steinberg in an Arnold Scaasi, Mrs. Paul Hallingby in an Ungaro, Mrs. Guilford Dudley, Mrs. Thomas Kempner and Mrs. Oscar Wyatt all in Saint Laurents, Mrs. T. Suffern Tailer in an Adolfo, Mrs. Robert Trump in a Lacroix, Mrs. Milton Petrie in another Scaasi, Carolina Herrera in a Carolina Herrera, Mary McFadden in a Mary McFadden and the Baroness de Portanova in a de la Renta, and so forth;

Tiffany's great jewelry designer Elsa Peretti dances in the Versailles Room of the St. Regis at the 1975 Platt party.

but no one but the guests have seen the magical wonderlands decked out with avalanches of Casablanca lilies, geysers of gypsophila, roadblocks of roses and eruptions of euphorbia inhabited by these *grande dame* fund-raisers, all glittering with success and glowing in the spotlight.

Tiffany Parties is an all-American portrait of these wonderlands of splendor where all sense of proportion is lost, where wealth hobnobs with poetry and ostentation with charity, and where there is as little relation to reality as possible. These are ultimately sophisticated gatherings, irresistibly seductive, hopelessly romantic; fleeting mirages of paradise as evanescent as the wealth, power and pride that bring them into being. They have the pomp and ritual of coronations, the festivity of royal weddings, the bravado of cavalry charges, and the gaiety of carnivals. They are filled with a taste for joy and astonishment which for a few rejuvenating hours cuts life's problems down to a very small size.

Big parties are a world built not only of legend, money, social clout and tax-deductible contributions, but of imagination and fantasy. Their theatrical lighting, flowers, topiaries, candles, balloons, linens, crystals, porcelains and silvers can be bewitching when orchestrated by the masterful hands of America's party designers such as Robert Isabell, John Funt, Marlo, Clive David, Don Bolen, Peggy Mulholland, or Preston Bailey.

Where the "shelter" press made interior designers the heroes of the decorative arts in the decade from 1975 to 1985, the party designers, those conjurers of the sumptuous and the hectic, have in the last five years taken a place beside them as celebrities of American design. Their accomplishment is to have given celebrations a new look and life here in the United States where, unlike Europe, the frivolities of society are as a rule tempered by philanthropic urges. Unlike their European equivalents, they do not take place in the great palaces of an aristocracy. Costumed international society surrounded by the splendors of Paris's Hôtel Lambert or by the Tiepolo frescoes of the Palazzo Labia in Venice needs little further décor. Our designers' settings shown here in *Tiffany Parties* are the palaces of the people: museums, libraries, opera houses, hotels, train stations, tents in public parks. It is the settings, not the guests, which are costumed.

Great American parties balance charity and civilizing moments of goodwill and refinement amidst the hubbub and irritations of modern life, rekindling *joie de vivre* in our society.

John Loring
New York
5 Jan 1989

William F. Buckley, Jr., poses for society photographers with Mrs. Thomas Kempner on his right and his wife Pat on his left.

Introduction

A silver tureen crammed with pink roses shimmers in the center of the gleaming mahogany of a Georgian dining table. Each opalescent petal blows open until the fat blossoms flutter in the candlelight. Languidly they drop apart until, by midnight, a dusting of petals lies amidst the crumbs and clutter of dessert.

Parties, from a backyard family reunion to an opulent operatic ball, manifest our most basic rituals and ardent aspirations. The fantasy, the security, the affirmation of fortune and position fuel every invitation, every placement, every toast and cheer.

And that explains the twenty-five thousand dollars someone pays for the great bowl of ice-pink roses sent to the table of America's new fortunes by New York florist Marlo. What madness, what folly to pay an unspeakable sum for something so fragile and ephemeral as an overheated rose! That rose, tied with the silken cords that bind Marlo to her expectant customers, unlocks the mystery of the grand party: for a few hours, magic is the rule. Everyone is beautiful, everyone is rich, and everyone is happy; a sitting room is a salon filled with the cleverest artists and the noblest patrons. Merchant bankers become merchant princes and their wives become courtesans. It's all time for make-believe.

Parties mirror their times, reflecting symbols of class, prosperity, art and fashion. They embody the very personality of an age. In the Venetian Republic's heady atmosphere of charm and sensual refinement, the most polished guests might contribute exotic cloves, olives or even a fine grayling to the dinner. "Never arrive empty-handed" remains an Italian maxim. Today, to carry along a fish, however rare and tasty, to dinner at Mrs. Astor's would be out of place; but tucking a quarto of sonnets in the style of a *settecento* prince into your pocket might well enhance your popularity.

In America in the eighties the sheer immensity of accumulation and accomplishment makes entertaining possible on a vastly extravagant scale. Spending, in Post-industrial America, is an industry in itself. The breakthrough, within the last eight years, has been the $1,000 charity ticket. Pay it once, and you'll pay it three times a week.

These luxuriously extravagant entertainments are a metaphor for a culture that, with its rage for trends and transition, has evaded being characterized by a focused image. We build to replace, we reek with bold and factitious power, and to celebrate all this we have invented a completely capricious and brash fashion for parties, which has produced an entirely new social order.

(Opposite) *Social arbiter Jerry Zipkin dances with Nan Kempner at the 1980 Platt Ball to the music of Brian McKenna and the Cliff Hall Orchestra. His Lucite cane, he explained to Jane Lane of W, was "for protection."*

(Above) *Mr. Joseph H. Lauder and Estée Lauder pose at the entrance to the 1980 Platt Ball decorated in neo-Egyptian style by John Loring. Queen of beauty authorities Mrs. Lauder commented on the evening, "Everyone made an effort to look pretty, which is unusual."*

Pat Buckley, the New Yorker who may most easily qualify as a socialite—but with a piquant twist—has said that she works so energetically organizing charity galas because, not being terribly rich, her contribution is service.

Pat Buckley, under the aegis of Diana Vreeland, has worked since 1978 on the Costume Institute galas at the Metropolitan Museum of Art, plumbing the depths of Manhattan with designer John Funt for plastic lampshades to be gilded with spray paint, begging for Lurex from textile manufacturers, reshaping the immutable cafeteria of the Met with billowing lamé for a party that in a few hours raises millions for the museum.

Surely record amounts are flowing into the coffers of charities (and their professional benefit arrangers), but the industry has also created a galaxy of stars whose names or presence emit an alluringly seductive glow. The nebulae form into various special-interest groups—lovers of real estate, of books, of music, of hospitals and of the homeless. Their social diversity is great: borrowers and lenders, designers and decorators, merchants and traders and the linchpins—women, those grappling up the social cliffs, or those twisting painfully as they hang on to the heights. Party giving is a business in which women have remarkable power, economic, political, and social.

The key to a successful party is a team: Pat Buckley and John Funt at the Metropolitan Museum of Art, Nancy Reagan and her outstanding White House organization, Carroll Petrie and Marlo. These teams merge the establishment with the energetic New Rich, reserved aristocrats with neon celebrities, and brew up an extravaganza of paparazzi madness, of political scheming for desirable seating, and in the case of the Metropolitan, of visibility for a museum that faces the whole carnival with occasional faintheartedness. The Seventh Avenue fashion world, with its style and brassy panache, has stormed and captured the once sacred precincts of the Met.

The Costume Institute gala was the inspired creation of Diana Vreeland, brilliant former fashion editor, Special Consultant to the Costume Institute, and one of the most visually gifted and dramatic personalities of our age. Seventh Avenue and Park Avenue merged at her behest, and she truly can be said to have ushered in this New Age of parties. The museum became a gladiatorial arena of giving, and one of the privileges (beyond the desired publicity) of substantial check-writing is the use of the museum's rooms for parties. Corporate sponsorship for a few tens of thousands of dollars enables the donor to use the museum for one night, and the glittering Temple of Dendur, the crystalline John Roche-Kevin Dinkeloo wing, goes to work in the service of arbitrageurs and buyout kings.

As the Costume Institute party at the Metropolitan shepherded in change, the Literary Lions gala at the New York Public Library resisted it, holding attendance down and prices up. The notorious $1,000 ticket was born here. But as the diamantine brilliance of the Met's new rooms fits a correspondingly glittering crowd, the warmly grand Beaux Arts atmosphere of the Carrère and Hastings library attracts a more solidly based constituency.

As the characters in the play have changed, so have the props. Dinner for eight hundred in a hotel ballroom was once an ordeal of chicken with a beige sauce, a potato, limp broccoli and cloyingly sweet chocolate mousse with a swizzle of pressurized whipped cream. A fellow named Sean Driscoll, with his partner at the time, Christopher Idone, initiated a shift away from professional, permanent in-house staffs, with their relentlessly dull menus, and wafted a new American flavor into the air. A different, public and totally indigenous group—neither American Old Guard nor European—was making its mark, and making pot roast and apple crisp, all cooked and served with astonishing élan, the epitome of chic.

What Driscoll did was to take the austere but sound values of the wobbly gentry and stamp them with luxury, style and faultless service. There is something rather startling at New York parties about the battalion of Glorious Food waiters in formation—all seemingly from central casting—pristine in dinner jackets and impeccable white gloves.

But all contemporary entertaining does not take place in vast public arenas with dinners for one thousand, the ladies decked in the entire annual production of De Beers, and miles of silk taffeta. Although the headiness of achieving social success and visibility that public charity galas provide dominates most parties, people still have babies and birthdays and want to celebrate the Fourth of July.

The purpose of a party is to celebrate, whether for your first billion, or for your first grandchild. Let's say it's *not* a glamorous, champagne-soaked, starlit poolside party in Bel Air. Let's say it's *not* lunch for 120 on the North Shore of Long Island; so, the canapés will be Ritz crackers with a bit of cheese spread, the wine a slightly sticky white not too chilled, and the tomato bisque tinned and not too hot. Let's say we're not back in a hotel ballroom dancing for another disease where someone is celebrating having $5,000 to pay for a table, enough friends to fill it, a wife who will look very pleasant indeed in chiffon, and, well, you get the picture. It can still be every bit as celebratory as a Labor Day lobster lunch in a Newport "cottage," and it will undoubtedly be relaxed and probably fun.

The problem you would face, however, if you were in that dreamed-of hotel ballroom seated beside your billionaire host is what to say. The real

(Above, top) *Princess Manni of Sayn-Wittgenstein-Sayn dances with Prince Edouard de Lobkowicz with Earl Blackwell in the background at a Platt ball.*

(Above, bottom) *Among Harry Platt's glamorous guests at his 1980 ball were Anglo-American royals Mr. and Mrs. John R. Drexel III, shown here between Franco-Viennese-American royals Prince and Princess Edouard de Lobkowicz.*

At the same Platt party, film star Merle Oberon chats with Princess Lalanezha, sister of Morocco's King Mohamed V.

estate developer Donald Trump confessed to the intrepid conversationalist seated to his left one night—to his "charmer," in party parlance—that there was little that interested him apart from business. He is not, he confessed, secretly obsessed with Russian furniture (they were, on this occasion, not in the Plaza ballroom but at Sotheby's, a now popular venue for parties in New York). What real estate developers are usually quite openly obsessed with is square feet. Conversation is a territory where square feet don't count, but for any dinner companion who wants to make the effort, thinking fast while sitting down is an invaluable asset; and in this world of celebration assets count.

The engagés in this social enterprise work, and work hard and long, for a living—the men and, increasingly, the women. They're up early and prefer to go to bed early; they can be rather testy and high-strung, as they are frequently awaiting millions and sometimes billions in financing, or faxed documents from their lawyers, or face the crisis of unkind publicity in the business press, which has, at moments, forged a queer alliance with the social press. They are not, in short, the eternally young debonair, hard-living, hard-drinking playboys of the twenties, thirties or forties who weren't afraid of staggering out of bed at eleven, dressing for luncheon and lurching—head pounding—to "21" for the cure. Long nights at El Morocco, when dinner was accompanied by whiskey, not wine, and short rides home along a still-residential Park Avenue have been superseded by a more austere schedule determined primarily by work.

Today's *grande dame* reads the business weeklies before a dinner party. The young social contender debriefs her husband on the latest and hottest deals on Wall Street in order to be more seductive over the raspberry soufflé. The placement stew will generally be seasoned with a writer, of sorts, or a museum specialist, of sorts, perhaps a dancer (retired); but this is a device generally employed only for decorative effect or to titillate the old and restless. It is all easy, dictated by formula, geared to the brief attention span of the contemporary elite.

The natural ebullience of the American social creature has produced an appropriate technique of entertaining.

Parties, all magical and wonderful, achieve the height of fantasy in hard-boiled, hard-driven times when romantic escape at the most means watching Blake Carrington present Krystle with a diamond bracelet. Proust may haunt the parties of the nostalgic French, but Americans have no part of it. Forward-looking and earnest, Americans are free of the mist of melancholy that veils the great French parties, or the decadence of the English, or the disarray of the Italians. The dashing originality of Americans is eminently suited to having fun.

John Travolta dances with the Princess of Wales at the White House, and the world watches.

Jane Lane

At his 1969 ball Harry Platt dances with the Duchesse D'Uzes (the former Peggy Bancroft).

New York Public Library Ten Treasures Dinner

America knows no more magnificent public spaces than the halls of the New York Public Library designed by architects Carrère and Hastings and opened on May 24, 1911.

Here on May 19, 1988, in two of its grand interiors the library hosts its annual dinner to benefit its General Book Fund.

Just beyond the great entrance hall in the D. Samuel and Jeane H. Gottesman Exhibition Hall's cavernous 6,400-square-foot space punctuated with four Renaissance-style cipollino marble arches, interior designer Mark Hampton covered the tables of ten with his own "Anabel" flowered chintz and had Mädderlake florists create massive centerpieces of peonies, roses, lilacs and Queen Anne's lace. The stone urns in arches and alcoves carried out the triumphantly floral theme with more Mädderlake compositions of giant delphiniums, calla lilies, day lilies, Casablanca lilies, French roses, dogwood and azaleas.

Downstairs under the 30-foot-high glass dome of the cavernous Celeste

Bartos Forum, with its graceful cast iron architecture and yellow and gray Siena marble walls inlaid with bronze acanthus bells, interior designer Suzie Frankfurt set a magical mood in silver and white. Massed papery white Casablanca lilies arranged by celebrated floral designer Robert Isabell sat close to the pale gray ottoman-silk-covered tables and bathed in the light of vigil candles. In the center of the forum a unique 600-pound, 7-foot-tall Rockwood art pottery vase held a

majestic Robert Isabell composition of white dogwood and flowering plum towering a breathtaking twenty feet above the floor.

The library's guests dined on Glorious Foods' Asparagus Mornay, Apple Smoked Turkey Breast with Cumberland Sauce, and Angel Food Cake with Caramel Ice Cream.

The Ten Treasures Dinner was chaired by Mrs. Donald Newhouse. Honorary Chairmen were Mrs. Vincent Astor and Annette Reed.

Irving Berlin's 100th Birthday, New York

*O*n the evening of Wednesday May 11, 1988, ASCAP, the American Society of Composers, Authors, and Publishers, and Carnegie Hall threw a benefit 100th birthday party for America's greatest songwriter, Irving Berlin.

In a birthday salute to Berlin, President Reagan wrote from the White House that "his immortal songs have cheered us, thrilled us, rallied us, and gladdened us. Today and always we salute this great composer, this great American, the man who gave his adopted country 'God Bless America'."

The star-studded birthday celebrants paid up to a thousand dollars a ticket for the best seats at the Carnegie Hall salute and the best tables at the post-concert dinner in the New York Hilton's grand ballroom, patriotically decorated in red, white and blue by Tiffany & Co.'s Director of Display and celebrated party designer John Funt, in a "Top Hat, White Tie and Tails" mood.

At the concert, Berlin's famous friends and well-wishers sang their favorites chosen from his fifteen hundred songs. Frank Sinatra sang

"Always" and "When I Lost You." Ray Charles sang "How Deep Is the Ocean," Shirley MacLaine belted "No Business Like Show Business," Marilyn Horne sang "God Bless America," Tony Bennett sang "Let's Face the Music and Dance," Rosemary Clooney sang "White Christmas." Leonard Bernstein sang "Russian Lullaby," Willie Nelson "Blue Skies," Nell Carter "Alexander's Ragtime Band," Tommy Tune "Puttin' on the Ritz." Natalie Cole belted "I Love a Piano"—and so on into the night.

The benefit committee, which included Mrs. Fred Astaire, Mrs. Bing Crosby, Mrs. Ira Gershwin, Mrs. Kitty Carlisle Hart, Mrs. Richard Rogers, Miss Beverly Sills, Mrs. Isaac Stern and Mrs. Marietta Tree, and their guests dined on Grilled Veal Chops with Asparagus Polonaise and Chocolate Top Hats

Filled with White Chocolate Mousse and decorated with white gloves, Irving Berlin's initials and a cane.

The New York Philharmonic Ball

*W*hile *"Top Hat, White Tie and Tails"* spirit reigned a few blocks south at Irving Berlin's 100th birthday party, nine hundred other revelers celebrated *"A Night in Venice"* at the New York Philharmonic's splendid masked ball held in a vast tent-cum-Venetian-palace in Lincoln Center's Damrosch Park.

A trumpet fanfare heralded the arrival of the guests, many disguised in extravagant celebrity-designed masks auctioned by Sotheby's on February 29th after a benefit cocktail party showing at Tiffany & Co.'s Fifth Avenue store. Tiffany's also provided the invitations for the ball.

At tables decorated with airborne bouquets of pale pink and white peonies, stock and miniature orchids, guests dined on Glorious Food's menu of Antipasto Misto, Lombata di Vitello Ripieno, Orzo con Porcini, Caponata and Zuppa Inglese di Palazzo.

Honorary ball chairman Zubin Mehta led the New York Philharmonic in the evening's theme, the overture to A Night in Venice *by* Johann Strauss, Jr., *followed by* Ziehrer's *"Fächer"* polonaise and more Strauss, the *"Voices of Spring"* and the *"Tritsch-Tratsch"* polka. The evening continued with more music for dancing by Michael Carney and his orchestra.

The event, which was chaired by Mrs. Evan G. Galbraith, Mrs. Gordon P. Getty and Mrs. Jon A. Wurtzburger raised one million dollars for the Philharmonic.

An Evening with Calvin Klein to Benefit the Ellington Fund, Washington, D.C.

The daunting scale of Washington's Old Pension Building, now the National Building Museum, with its dizzying 159-foot ceiling gives it a majestic, authoritarian splendor reminiscent of the Byzantine Empire.

Grover Cleveland first recognized its potential as a place to have a ball and, two years before its opening, held his Inaugural Ball there in 1885.

On June 15, 1988, Nordstrom's department stores and American fashion sultan Calvin Klein gave a party for six hundred and sixty to benefit Washington's Duke Ellington School of the Arts. Six sheer white silk curtains were hung between the Great Hall's eight 8-by-75-foot marbleized Corinthian columns (the world's largest Corinthian columns, each built of 70,000 bricks). The hall's central fountain was turned into a garden of white delphiniums, agapanthus, calla lilies and roses by "court decorator" Robert Isabell, who

filled the centers of the white-clothed tables with his signature massed Casablanca lilies covering chicken wire-wrapped crystal bowls.

Peter Duchin and his orchestra played.

Mrs. Katharine Graham and Ms. Peggy Cooper Cafritz and Mr. Jason S. Berman were Honorary Chairman and Co-chairmen.

Calvin Klein premiered his Fall 1988 collection.

Leading Washington caterer Design Cuisine's Jordan Gipple and

chef Horst Klein offered Salmon Ravigote with Shallot Sauce, Grilled Wild Pheasant and Mango Ice.

The Ellington School, founded in 1968, provides nearly six hundred students with opportunity for academic excellence and artistic proficiency.

The Nelson A. Rockefeller Public Service Award Dinner, New York

*F*ew rooms have so often played host to the party-going as the Grand Ballroom of New York's fabled Waldorf-Astoria Hotel. Here on June 16, 1988, in its suave and streamlined American Deco interior, the first Nelson A. Rockefeller Public Service Award Dinner honored former majority leader of the U.S. Senate, and since 1977 our ambassador to Japan, Mike Mansfield.

The more than one thousand guests included Mrs. Nelson (Happy) Rockefeller, Nelson Jr. and Mark Rockefeller, the Laurance Rockefellers, Governor Cuomo, Lauren Bacall, Nancy Kissinger, Senator Daniel Moynihan, the Robert Mosbachers, and former New York mayors Abe Beame, Robert Wagner and John Lindsay.

Leading New York party designer Robert Isabell decorated the ballroom with baskets of pink and white peonies illuminated from all sides with candles.

The Waldorf-Astoria's executive chef John Doherty served Curried Tomato and Zucchini Soup, Tournedos of Beef with Béarnaise Sauce, Oven-Roasted Potatoes with Rosemary, Tomato and Purée of Broccoli and Fresh Asparagus accompanied by New York State wines, followed by Strawberries and Champagne Truffles.

Lionel Hampton and his orchestra provided dance music.

Ambassador Mansfield reminded everyone that public service is not just an extracurricular activity.

All proceeds from the dinner benefited the Nelson A. Rockefeller Institute of Government at the State University of New York (SUNY).

Mrs. John Kluge's Birthday Party, New York

To honor his wife Patricia's birthday, Metromedia's John Kluge held a white-tie and tails dinner on September 17, 1988, in a metamorphosed Grand Ballroom of the Waldorf-Astoria. Delighting guests, Los Angeles party architect Clive David transformed the space into a Viennese ballroom with unexpected British overtones.

A million flowers—roses, stephanotis, freesia, bouvardia, lilies and orchids decorated the tables and a gigantic chandelier. Ropes of flowers hung from the upper tiers of boxes. Mel Atlas, the floral expert, designed gilt wrought-iron candelabra rising 6 feet above each table, crowned with eighteen shaded candle lights and covered at the base with great bursts of flowers. The existing Waldorf chandelier was increased five times its size with cascades of crystal teardrops interspersed with more flowers.

Waldorf Executive Chef Jim Doherty's first course was a Vol-au-Vent of Lobster, Shrimp and Crab with Watercress Sauce, and a 1986 Chardonnay from the Kluges' Virginia vineyard. The rest of the dinner was served from a European

hunt table featuring decorative wild game, Alaska king crab, saddlery, hunting gear, fruits and flowers. There were great assortments of seafood along with tureens of Marinated Squab and Foie Gras, Quail with Quail Eggs and Roast Suckling Pig.

The Bob Hardwick Orchestra played music for dancing. Four ballerinas presented birthday cakes, designed by New York queen of cake design Sylvia Weinstock. There were three hundred and sixty guests, nine for each of Mrs. Kluge's forty years.

The Opening of the New York Central Park Zoo

*F*our hundred guests—dubbed "the Zoo 400"— attended the late June 1988 opening of the new Central Park Zoo held in a transparent tent pitched by Chris Starr amongst the zoo's colonnades.

Party-decorating lion John Funt placed forty purple-and-burgundy fuchsias in forty neoclassic Tiffany ceramic pots as centerpieces and surrounded them with hurricane globes sheltering crystal dolphin candlesticks from Tiffany's "Treasures from Stately Homes Collection."

Mrs. Vincent Astor—who founded the Women's Committee of the New York Zoological Society after an escaped concave-casqued hornbill, which she named Vera, landed on her terrace—honorarily co-chaired the evening along with Mrs. Charles A. Dana, Jr., Mrs. Enid A. Haupt, Mrs. Jack R. Howard, Mrs. Charles W. Nichols, Jr., Mrs. Harmon L. Remmel, and Mrs. Joseph A. Thomas.

Mrs. Richard T. Perkin was chairman.

Mrs. Rand Araskog, Mrs. Charles Hickox and Mrs. Gordon Pattee co-chaired.

The zoo's penguins, polar bears and sea lions greeted the guests.

Glorious Foods provided glorious food.

Bob Hardwick's orchestra played glorious music.

Tiffany & Co. provided the invitations as well as table favors— sterling key rings engraved with the Women's Committee's symbol, the bird named Vera that so adroitly visited Mrs. Astor.

Ambassador and Countess Wachtmeister's Dinner, Washington, D.C.

*T*he delightful wife of Sweden's ambassador to the United States, Countess Ulla Wachtmeister, is a long-acknowledged leader of Washington society and the diplomatic community. Here in the Swedish Embassy on Nebraska Avenue she sets a lavish Swedish cold buffet for a reception in honor of the chiefs of diplomatic missions.

The Count and Countess Wachtmeister's 250 guests will enjoy the much-acclaimed cuisine of Bjarne Åberg, the thirty-three-year-old embassy chef who, this late June evening, has prepared Marinated Salmon with Mustard Sauce, Pickled Duck with Apples, Prunes and Red Cabbage, Smoked Reindeer, small Pancakes Filled with Swedish Caviar, Spinach Pancakes with Crabmeat Filling, Marinated Asparagus, Cabbage Dolmas with Lingonberries, Fish Pâté with Dill Sauce, Rhubarb Pie, Petits Fours and Fruitcakes, to name only a few of the buffet's many-splendored delights.

Red roses from the embassy garden are held in ormolu Empire baskets by ormolu cherubs. The baskets and cherubs, like the cut-crystal tiered épergnes and mirrored plateau centerpiece, were purchased in Napoleonic Paris by Countess Wachtmeister's great, great, great-grandfather, who was Governor of Stockholm and who doubtless would have felt totally at home with this setting of mixed abundance, panache and good-natured grandeur.

His great, great, great-granddaughter muses on Swedish hospitality: "Informality with elegance, lots of good food with some surprises, masses of flowers and lots of candles, all create an atmosphere of relaxed enjoyment."

On summer evenings, she notes, "Even the fireflies help with a thousand points of light!"

Mrs. Virginia S. Milner's Hawaiian Luau Honoring Mr. and Mrs. Walter Annenberg, Beverly Hills

The coasts of Southern California and Hawaii joined forces on the evening of August 13th, 1988, for a gala poolside dinner for sixty in the lavishly Hollywooded Beverly Hills garden of leading Los Angeles hostess Virginia Milner to honor publisher and former Ambassador to the Court of St. James Walter Annenberg and Mrs. Annenberg.

Leading Los Angeles party producer/scriptwriter/designer/ director Stanley R. Kersten created a tropical paradise of Hawaiian orchids, miniature pineapples, frangipanis, celosia, ginger and bird of paradise flowers springing up from centerpieces and five miniature tropical gardens floating on the sky-blue waters of the Milner pool.

Tables were covered with bright tropical-colored leaf prints and set with multicolored napkins, Trader Vic's "Tiki" salt and peppers,

Tiffany sterling silver "Palm" candlesticks and menu cards in bird of paradise colors announcing the Trader Vic's menus of Kawai Cold Soup with Croutons in Wikiwiki Shells; Indonesian Lamb, Tahitian Barbecued Squab, Pahe Noodles, Taro Baskets with Vegetables; Rum Ice Cream with Pralines; Coffee Grog; Wine and Beer.

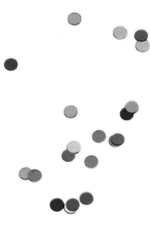

Mrs. Lawrence Copley Thaw's Dinner in Honor of Mrs. Guilford Dudley, Jr., New York

*A*t a formal spring dinner for thirty-two honoring Mrs. Guilford Dudley, Jr., of Palm Beach and Nashville, Mrs. Lawrence Copley Thaw called on party designer John Funt to create an intimately festive, spring-colored mood filled with grace and charm in keeping with the eighteenth-century French stylishness of her vast Park Avenue maisonette. Sixteen gilded bamboo ballroom chairs are alternated with Mrs. Thaw's Louis XVI dining room chairs, effectively echoing the Tiffany vermeil "Bamboo" flatware Mrs. Thaw uses at parties.

The tables' white cloths provided a fresh background for eighteenth-century Vieux-Paris porcelains decorated with small sprays of blue flowers.

Massive Venetian crystal baluster candlesticks made for Tiffany & Co. by Archimede Seguso held John Funt's explosive bouquets of white and pink peonies and champagne roses accented with stems of pink ixia.

Miniature bouquets of other pastel-colored spring flowers and votive candles sat beneath the taller arrangements along with the menus in Mrs. Thaw's handwriting for the dinner of Mousse de Crevettes—Sauce Choron, Carré d'Agneau Vert Pré, Charlotte au Chocolat Blanc-framboise.

Arriving in Mrs. Thaw's marble entrance hall, guests were greeted by a bust by the great eighteenth-century French sculptor Jean-Antoine Houdon of his daughter, on a gilt Louis XVI console which surveyed the

seating arrangement cards, also in Mrs. Thaw's handwriting. Seating thirty-two she finds as diplomatically intricate a task as seating five hundred at the glittering dinners she frequently orchestrates for Sotheby's in New York.

Mr. and Mrs. Milton Petrie's Fourth of July Party, Southampton

*F*ew names appear as frequently as chairman or co-chairman of New York's great society benefit balls as Mrs. Milton Petrie's. No one knows better the subtleties of seating a table of ten or a box at the opera; and the surprise eightieth-birthday dinner the ever beautiful and ever sociable Carroll Petrie threw for her chain-store-czar husband in the Charles Engelhard Courtyard of the Metropolitan Museum in 1987 remains a standard by which all subsequent New York private parties are judged.

Here in their Southampton home, the Petries celebrate the Fourth of July with a smaller private dinner for forty which also celebrates their friend Aileen Mehle ("Suzy" to her public), who said of the evening, "It was of such beauty, I cannot begin to tell you."

New York's reigning magician/conjurer of floral fantasies and their accessories, Marlo Phillips, was responsible as she so often is at Petrie parties for creating the Fourth

of July flowerworks. "She is something special," notes Mrs. Petrie.

Floral topiary trees mixing American flags, fruit, flowers, candy, feather birds, lace, ribbons, toy animals and silk fringes sat on tablecloths of lace-ruffled chintz surrounded and invaded by Tiffany silver, crystal and porcelain candlesticks of every description holding candles of every color.

"This, like everything I do, has nothing to do with anything but the

positive beauty and energy of the approaching 1990s," Marlo clairvoyantly notes.

Glorious Foods served a dinner of Small Artichoke Bottoms Filled with Caviar; Shrimp and Long Island Bay Scallops; Leek, Zucchini and Carrot Vinaigrette; Marinated Stuffed Roast Loin of Pork with Fresh Corn, Sweet Potatoes with Marshmallows and Lemon Rind, and Blueberry Cobbler with Vanilla Ice Cream.

Walter Gubelmann's Eightieth Birthday Party, Newport

The most gilded ballroom of America's Gilded Age was designed for Newport's Marble House by Richard Morris Hunt and inaugurated in 1892 by its proud possessors, Mr. and Mrs. William K. Vanderbilt.

Here, some years later on June 18, 1988, under the massive twin chandeliers copied by Hunt from originals at Château Maisons-Laffitte, the Gold Ballroom of The Preservation Society of Newport County's Marble House plays host to a formal dinner dance for 110 friends given by Mrs. Walter ("Barton") Gubelmann to fête her husband on his eightieth birthday.

Birthday partyers dined on Seafood en Gelée, Rack of Lamb in Cumberland Sauce, Ratatouille, Pommes de Terre, Coconut Cake Palm Beach and Raspberry Sorbet prepared by Steven Renshaw, chef at Newport's White Horse Tavern.

Raspberry pink was the color of the evening. Tables were covered with raspberry pink tablecloths and gold

mesh overlays by New York and Palm Beach party designer Harry Deal Bell. Bell also created centerpieces of tall glass vases filled with raspberry pink jelly beans and topped with explosive bouquets of lilies, peonies, irises, pink gerberas, orchids, ferns, delphiniums and pink ostrich plumes. Raspberry-pink ribbons tied to the backs of silvered ballroom chairs held raspberry-pink balloons.

Guests at Mr. Gubelmann's table ate from cobalt-blue-and-gold antique Minton china and drank from gilded antique crystal stemware, all originally from Tiffany & Co.

There were pink-and-silver birthday "crackers" filled with noisemakers and paper hats for all.

The Neil Smith Orchestra played for the dancing-minded in the palatial main entrance hall, the scene ninety-three years before of Consuelo Vanderbilt's coming-out party.

The Tiffany Feather Ball, New York

*F*rom the day New York's great showplace, the Plaza Hotel, opened in 1907 it took its place as an American institution, and it was here that in 1966 Truman Capote's Black and White Ball opened a new era in American parties.

The Plaza's neighboring American institution, Tiffany & Co., fittingly chose to give its 1988 Tiffany Feather Ball in the Plaza's ballroom, a triumph of the pillared and gilded "Louis l'Hôtel" American palace style.

At this Tiffany ball benefiting Just One Break, a leader in rehabilitation of the disabled, Mrs. Ronald Reagan served as honorary chairman and Mrs. Guilford Dudley, Jr., as chairman.

The May 24th dinner dance was designed by Tiffany's Director of Interior Display John Funt around an Elizabethan May Day theme with lime, pink, yellow and white Maypole streamers mixed with garlands of Tivoli lights everywhere.

The tables were covered in mixed pastel cloths and the ballroom chairs slipcovered in a striped toile. Each table had a flowering lantana tree centerpiece. The lantanas were set in unpainted pine tubs, their bases surrounded with arrangements of Elizabethan weeds, yellow marigolds, daisies and dried wheat animated with small colorful feather birds.

Just One Breakers dined on the Plaza executive chef's menu of Timbale of Salmon and Trout Mousse with Mustard Tarragon Sauce, Cornish Game Hen with Spaghetti Squash, Asparagus Tips and Cauliflower au Gratin, and French Vanilla Ice Cream with Hot Minted Bittersweet Chocolate Sauce.

The Tiffany Feather Ball
Just One Break, Inc.
The Plaza Hotel
Tuesday, May 24th, 1988
Reception 7:30 o'clock
The Terrace Room
Dinner 9:00 o'clock
The Grand Ballroom
Black tie

The Swan Ball, Nashville

In a burst of color worthy of the Tennessee Botanical Gardens and the Fine Arts Center at Nashville's Cheekwood, which it benefits, the 26th annual Swan Ball was held on June 11, 1988.

Above the men in white tie with their ladies dressed for the occasion in green, blue, yellow and poppy-red gowns, giant laminated paper lilies and poppies blossomed on faux trees, all designed by party designer Roberta Lochte.

Tables centered on florist Joe Smith's 2-foot-tall crystal "Chinese" vases filled with Connecticut king lilies, white agapanthus, pink peonies, purple liatris, red amaryllis and blue delphinium.

Caterer Charles Kates created a menu for the eight hundred guests of Cheese Salad, Tournedos of Beef with Shiitake and Chanterelle Mushroom Sauce served with Potato Pancakes, Jerusalem Artichokes Topped with Parmesan Cheese, Tomatoes Stuffed with Herbed Bread Crumbs and a Triple Chocolate Timbale with Mandarin Orange Slices Dipped in Chocolate.

The Marshall Grant Orchestra played. Carolyne Roehm showed her early fall fashion collection. Mrs. George W. Crook and Mrs. Ansel L. Davis chaired and co-chaired. The Swan Award went to John Howard Dobkin, director of the National Academy of Design in New York, in appreciation of his significant contributions to the arts. Mr. Dobkin was applauded by all, including honorary chairman of the Swan Ball and Tiffany board member Mrs. Guilford Dudley, Jr., and his fellow New Yorkers Jerome Zipkin, Robert and Blaine Trump, and his popular wife, Inmaculada de Habsburgo y Lorena, President of the Spanish Institute.

The Southampton Hospital Ball

The Southampton Hospital Ball designer, *Vicente Wolf of Vicente Wolf & Associates Inc., found that the floral exuberance of parties can become too multicolored for hot summer evenings, so for the 1988 big event of the Hamptons' social season, the Southampton Hospital's annual summer fund-raiser held on August 13, he opted to limit his palette to a cooling white.*

The theme of the Hamptons is clearly the beach. Getting straight to the point, Wolf centered each white table surrounded by white folding chairs on miniature Long Island beach scenes, using white Styrofoam "sand," scallop shells, a short length of snow fence, Long Island beach dune grass and a variety of beachcombers' treasures—sand dollars, tiny sailboats, and wooden birds, all naturally painted white. He used white cloths and napkins, white china, white paper Japanese fans and white wine to combat the warm August evening.

Suspended in the three white tents high above the heads of the 1,640 Hamptonites, hundreds of illuminated white Japanese paper lanterns hung amidst garlands of

white netting and Tivoli lights to create a lyrically romantic mood.

Glorious Food served Tartlets of Shrimp and Apple, Tomato and Basil and Curried Chicken Salad with cocktails followed by a dinner of Apricot-Glazed Ham with Chutney Butter and Mustard, Pasta Primavera Vinaigrette, Potato Salad with Mussels and Black Truffles, and a variety of fruits and cheeses.

Chuck Scarborough of Southampton, the NBC-TV news anchorman, was master of ceremonies and introduced his sister-in-law and

the benefit evening's chairman, Charlotte Ford Downe.

The benefit is much enjoyed for its annual raffle, whose prizes live up to Southampton's standards. Mrs. Michel Bergerac won a jeweled bracelet; Mrs. J. Emmet Smith won a red hatchback Subaru; Jean Nada won a fur coat and Cindy Ronchetti won a barge trip down France's Marne River.

Guests dancing to the Bob Hardwick sound included Mrs. David Mahoney, Mrs. Rand Araskog, Chuck and Anne Scarborough, ball vice-chairman Anne Johnson and Deane Johnson, Bob Mackie, Peter and Jamee Gregory, Donald and Catie Marron, Jocelyn Javits, Pat and Marquette DeBary, and the last year's ball chairman, Jean Tailer.

Funds raised went to further the hospital's research into Lyme disease.

Blair House Tea Reception, Washington, D.C.

*U*nder the guidance of the Reagan administration's Chief of Protocol, Ambassador Selwa Roosevelt, and Curator Clement E. Conger, a three-year total renovation of Blair House, the White House's neighbor on Pennsylvania Avenue and the official guesthouse of the President of the United States, was completed in 1988.

This recent redecoration of the 112 rooms in the assemblage of four houses (the first built in 1824) was the work of New York interior design leaders Mario Buatta and Mark Hampton.

Here, at a summer reception for national officers of the American Society of Interior Designers held shortly after Blair House's reopening, guests were greeted by a vast silver Montieth bowl filled with agapanthus in the Press Reception Room where the President and visiting heads of state hold press conferences. The "Stately Homes of the British Isles Collections" furnishings in the Mark Hampton-decorated room were selected by English design impresario Sir Humphry Wakefield and include Baker furniture, Stroheim & Romann fabrics, Mottahedeh

ceramics and Karastan carpets.

ASIDers continued on into the Dillon Room, decorated by Mario Buatta with hand-painted eighteenth-century Chinese paper from Gracie.

A summer tea buffet of fruits and cakes and cookies was served in the Jackson Place Dining Room. New York party designer John Funt had decorated the table with two giant Tiffany French hand-painted faience vases holding sunflowers, agapanthus, roses, yarrow, bouvardia, sea holly and star of Bethlehem lilies. The tea was served with table furnishings designed and donated by Tiffany & Co. to Blair

House—"Blair House" pattern Pickard china, "English King" sterling flat silver and "Laurelton Hall" crystal stemware. The room's murals are by New York trompe-l'oeil painter Robert Jackson.

The center table of the neighboring front parlor held another John Funt composition of sunflowers, sea holly, ti leaves and yarrow. "Dolphin" crystal candlesticks from Tiffany's "Stately Homes Collection" completed the table.

"Every person who donated to the restoration," explained Ambassador Roosevelt, "has made a contribution to the foreign relations of the United States."

Lintas:
Worldwide

In Honor of
Senator and Mrs. Mark O.
And
Representative and Mrs. Stan
Thursday, July 14, 1988

Potage
Potage frais de Sorrenry
Cold sorrel soup

Poisson
Quenelles de crevettes avec un sauce d'homard
Shrimp quenelles with lobster sauce

Entrée
Suprêmes de volailles aux truffes et du champagne
Boneless breast of chicken with champagne and truffles

Salade
Salade verte au vinaigrette de framboises
Green salad with raspberry vinaigrette

Dessert
Panache de sorbet avec des fruits exotiques
Assorted sorbets with exotic fruits

Lintas Worldwide Reception, New York

On July 14, 1988, to honor Senator Mark Hatfield, Congressman Stephen Solarz and fourteen ambassadors of the Asian diplomatic corps in the United States, advertising giant Lintas Worldwide hosted a gala reception and dinner to foster greater dialogue between leading government and corporate players in Asia and the Pacific.

High above Manhattan at the #1 Dag Hammarskjold Plaza Lintas executive offices, guests dined on Lintas chef Katherine Keiffer's menu of Chilled Sorrel Soup, Shrimp Quenelles with Lobster Madeira Sauce, Chicken Fillets with Truffles, Timbales of Fennel, Assorted Fruit Sorbet and Chocolate Dacquoise Miniatures. The menu, an inspiration of Joel Seigle of Matheson Seigle Associates Public Relations, was a replica of one used by Queen Victoria for a luncheon reception honoring her youngest child, Princess Beatrice, on the occasion of her marriage to Prince Henry of Battenberg (grandfather of Prince Philip).

The party's opulent flower and fruit arrangements were designed by famed stylist Preston Bailey carrying out the Victorian theme with hydrangeas, orchids, flax, roses, sweet peas, delphiniums and lilies. Villeroy & Boch supplied a full service of one of their most popular china patterns, "Petite Fleur," and Tiffany & Co., who oversaw the evening's party design, lent some of its splendid and colorful crystal and ceramics for centerpieces as well as its "twinelights" to illuminate the New York summer evening.

The dinner was hosted by Lintas CEO William V. Weithas and Mrs. Weithas. The staggering guest list included: The Japanese UN ambassador, the Chinese ambassador, the ambassadors of Thailand, the Philippines, New Zealand, Pakistan, the ambassadors of Australia and Singapore to the UN, the chairman of Toshiba America, Nobuo Ishizaka, the chairman of Goldman Sachs International, Bob Hormats, Merrill Lynch chairman William Schreyer, Ralph Larsen, vice-chairman of Johnson & Johnson, and—as Suzy noted—"others too diplomatic and/or corporate to mention."

Green Animals Children's Picnic, Newport

*T*he Green Animals gardens of Newport, Rhode Island, contain over sixty boxwood topiary arches, globes, pyramids, urns, spirals and animals including a lion, a giraffe, birds, dogs, a donkey and a bear.

The estate was left to The Preservation Society of Newport in 1973 by Miss Alice Brayton, and here each summer The Preservation Society gives its annual lawn party for its members' children.

The children are entertained by clowns and jugglers, a puppet show, pony cart rides and music from a Dixieland band.

Hot dogs, lemonade, peanuts, and animal-shaped cookies donated by local residents are served to the youthful guests.

Mr. and Mrs. A. Leslie Bullard, who organize the event, provide a bar with more adult drinks for the parents.

Flowers selected from among the two hundred species that bloom in Green Animals' impressive beds were arranged by Mary T. Mendonça.

The Parrish Art Museum Dance, Southampton

*T*he invitation with a cover reproduction of Marsden Hartley's 1942 painting "Wild Roses" (on loan to Southampton's Parrish Art Museum from Washington's Phillips Collection) unorthodoxly announced "dresses: short and sassy" for the ladies and "blue blazers and white trousers" for the gentlemen.

The theme was "Wild Roses" for the Parrish benefit dance on Saturday, July 16th, 1988. To cover the fifty-four tables, interior designer Ronald Grimaldi of Rose Cumming supplied miles of rose-covered English "Patou" chintz, named in honor of haute-couturier Christian Lacroix (ex-of-Patou and fashion god of roses and the "short and sassy" look of summer 1988).

Interior designer Josef Pricci and Greg Yale of Greg Yale Landscape Illumination collaborated to create the enormous tent complete with Palladian windows and air conditioning that housed the affair.

Floral designer Diane Charkow of Chinadoxis gathered thousands of old-fashioned roses similar to those in Hartley's painting to create the evening's superb centerpieces.

Peter Duchin and his orchestra played and Denny Leroux sang for the guests including the evening's chairman, Mrs. Peter Stephen Gregory; and vice-chairmen, Mrs. L. Stoddard Horn and Mrs. Richard B. Nye; Carroll and Milton Petrie;

Karen and Richard LeFrak; Jonathan and Kimberly Farkas; Jean Suffern Tailer; Ahmet and Mica Ertegun; Pat and Marquette de Bary; Blaine and Robert Trump; Alessandro and Cathy di Montezemolo; Jerome Zipkin; Carolyne Roehm and Henry Kravis; Chessy and Bill Rayner, Mary and Michael Meehan, and others too wild and rosy to remember.

Glorious Foods provided a dinner of Pasta with Shrimp and Lemon Sauce, Cold Herbed Loin of Lamb with Mustard Sauce with Sweet Potato Salad with Pepper Confetti, and a Vacherin aux Fraises.

Tiffany & Co. provided favors of "Tiffany" fragrance and "Tiffany Ribbon" silk crêpe-de-chine scarves.

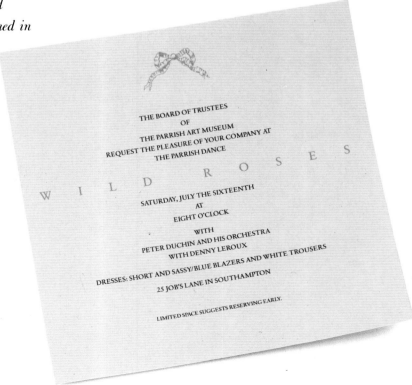

THE BOARD OF TRUSTEES
OF
THE PARRISH ART MUSEUM
REQUEST THE PLEASURE OF YOUR COMPANY AT
THE PARRISH DANCE

W I L D   R O S E S

SATURDAY, JULY THE SIXTEENTH
AT
EIGHT O'CLOCK

WITH
PETER DUCHIN AND HIS ORCHESTRA
WITH DENNY LEROUX

DRESSES: SHORT AND SASSY/BLUE BLAZERS AND WHITE TROUSERS

25 JOB'S LANE IN SOUTHAMPTON

LIMITED SPACE SUGGESTS RESERVING EARLY.

Bernstein at Seventy, Boston

*T*o benefit the Tanglewood Music Center, the Boston Symphony Orchestra threw a Gala Birthday Performance between two equally gala dinner parties to celebrate the seventieth birthday of composer, maestro and living legend Leonard Bernstein.

For the pre-concert gala supper at Lenox's Highwood Estate, party designer Barbara Bock Brader brought Berkshire Mountain wildflowers in to decorate two tents overlooking Stockbridge Bowl Lake. Her countrified yellow-and-white goldenrod and Queen Anne's lace compositions contrasted with navy blue tablecloths in keeping with the Wilds of Western Massachusetts theme for the dinner, which was catered by Stephen Elmot of Creative Gourmets in Boston. Pre-concerters enjoyed Grilled Chicken Salsa, Orzo Pilaf, Grilled Umbrian Vegetables, Salad of Field Greens and Chocolate Birthday Cakes with raspberry sauce.

At 8:30 the concert hosted by Beverly Sills, for which Bernstein enthusiasts had paid up to $5,000 for a ringside seat, began with Seiji Ozawa conducting the Boston Symphony in Bernstein's Chichester Psalms. More Bernstein followed: Michael Tilson Thomas conducted

the opening dance from Fancy Free; Betty Comden sang her lyrics of "One Hundred Easy Ways to Lose a Man" from Wonderful Town; Christa Ludwig sang "I Am Easily Assimilated" from Candide; Frederica Von Stade sang "A Little Bit in Love" from Wonderful Town; Larry Kert sang "Something's Coming" and Barbara Hendricks sang "I Feel Pretty," both from West Side Story; Yo-Yo Ma and Mstislav Rostropovich played the cello but not together; Victor Borge played the piano; Lauren Bacall sang Stephen

Sondheim's "The Saga of Lenny"; and President Reagan, as he had done three months earlier for Irving Berlin's 100th birthday, sent a letter from the White House. With the phrases of his earlier note fresh in his mind the President wrote, "From West Side Story to On the Waterfront, your music has cheered us, thrilled us, rallied us, gladdened us."

After the final notes of "Make Your Garden Grow" from Candide, which closed the Tanglewood concert, 485 performers and members of the

audience adjourned for dinner to the music room at Blantyre, Lenox's imposing tudor mansion-cum-inn, built in 1902 for turpentine king Robert Paterson and onetime possession of United Artists' D. W. Griffith, where an elaborate post-concert dinner was served.

Again Barbara Bock Brader decorated with arrangments of fruits, leaves and local wildflowers aided by some more cultivated lilies, and one buffet had a centerpiece featuring a marble flautist sitting in grapes, figs, strawberries, nectarines, lemon slices and bananas. His theme might also have been the Old Lady's tango from Candide, "I Am Easily Assimilated."

Bernstein's well-wishers assimilated Basil and Arugula with Auricchio and Parma Ham, Field Salad with French Icicle Radishes and Edible Wildflowers, Mixed Berries, Italian Cheeses, Reine de Saba Chocolate Almond Torte and a piano-shaped birthday cake of Chocolate Génoise and Nougatine, all prepared by Blantyre's executive chef, Steven Taub.

Ann Getty, Kitty Carlisle Hart and James Wolfensohn co-chaired the evening.

Back in the bedroom of Leonard Bernstein's home, a framed sampler comments, "If God had meant us to go to concerts, He'd have given us tickets."

Snowmass Picnic, Colorado

The Mosbacher ranch in the highland valley above Snowmass, Colorado, commands breathtaking panoramas of some of America's favorite ski runs: the expansive slopes of Big Burn, the rolling terrain of Elk Camp, the bumpier High Alpine, and the challenging Hanging Valley Wall.

Here where Ute Indians hunted elk and, later, pioneers using skis made out of barrel staves searched for silver, U.S. Secretary of Commerce Robert Mosbacher took time out one August afternoon from his 1988 marathon fund-raising blitz that raised staggering sums for the Bush presidential campaign for a fun-raising picnic with friends.

Secretary Mosbacher's dynamic all-American beauty wife Georgette, who is also Chairman and CEO of LaPrairie cosmetics, created a setting to match the majestic grandeur of the surrounding Rocky Mountains.

For her setting, which Mrs. Mosbacher laughingly titled "Georgette dans la Prairie," pale celadon green fluted antique Minton china originally belonging to Secretary Mosbacher's mother and originally from Tiffany & Co., New York, was placed on white eyelet embroidery place mats on the

setting's grass mat foundation. Oversized, heavily cut English crystal glasses joined the setting's theme of robust sophistication. Colorful Victorian porcelain flowers were pressed into service as place-card holders, while the center of the picnic setting was ornamented with small silver baskets of fresh fruits and mountain prairie wildflowers and small terra-cotta flowerpots of colorful candied fruits.

Sitting on overstuffed raw-silk-covered cushions, the Mosbachers' guests enjoyed a meal of Baked Texas Potatoes and Beluga Mallosol Caviar, Charcoal-Grilled Mountain Trout caught by Secretary Mosbacher

in his nearby mountain lake; Tomato, Texas Onion and Limestone Lettuce Salad; Corn on the Cob; and Spiced and Marinated Apples, Oranges, and Pears.

Champagne and sangría were served throughout the picnic, coffee and more champagne served at the neighboring Mosbacher hundred-year-old log cabin, decorated for the occasion with arrangements of Colorado mountain wildflowers, grasses and silvery green aspen leaves. The flowers included wild Rocky Mountain columbine, Colorado's state flower, yellow chamisa, yarrow, wild asters and a variety of thistles.

Cocktails Aboard *the* Trump Princess, *New York*

Mr. *and* Mrs. *Donald Trump's astonishing yacht measures in at an immodest 270 feet of polished steel, bronzed windows and technological refinements such as satellite guidance, three radars and an Atlas echo sounder. It boasts two 3,000-horsepower, 16-cylinder, turbocharged diesel engines. It was designed by London's Jon Bannenberg and built in Viareggio, Italy.*

Here for a late summer afternoon cocktail party for friends aboard the Trump Princess, anchored in New York's East River, admiral of party designers John Funt decorated the aft deck in shades of fuchsia and white using massed orchids accented with cockscomb and branches of flowering tropical kangaroo's paw.

Champagne was cooled in hand-painted Tiffany Private Stock porcelain wine coolers in Tiffany's black-and-gold "Nuits de Chine" pattern.

Guests at the "Nuit de New York" fête ate hors d'oeuvres from Tiffany's black-and-gold "Malmaison" plates with golden vermeil flatware.

On one of the small skirted tables scattered about the deck, a centerpiece assembled with orchids atop an overscale Venetian crystal dolphin candlestick by famed glassmaker Archimede Seguso lent another nautical touch.

The United Nations Building and the 59th Street Queensborough Bridge (neither as yet owned by Donald Trump) lent a New York-sized dimension to the setting in keeping with the dimensions of the Trump Princess.

The Atlanta Symphony Ball

*T*o toast the Atlanta Symphony's new thirty-nine-year-old Rumanian-born maestro, Yoel Levi, Joseph E. Seagram & Sons created "The Tiffany Blue Cocktail" mixed from 1 ounce Seagram's imported vodka, $\frac{1}{4}$ ounce Leroux Blue Curaçao, $\frac{1}{4}$ ounce fresh lemon juice and $\frac{1}{4}$ ounce peach schnapps, and garnished with a dendrobium orchid for this first Atlanta Symphony Ball, held on September 10, 1988.

After a seven o'clock concert held in Atlanta's Symphony Hall, the six hundred guests enjoyed hors d'oeuvres and Tiffany Blues at Atlanta's IBM Tower Gardens before dining in a circus-like tent, which somehow recalled the Sydney Opera House, inhabited by topiary moss and ivy lions by designer Barbara Gallup.

The lions held brass horns. The gold-lamé-covered tables held French-horn centerpieces filled with yellow, purple and white orchid sprays. There were miniature French horns for napkin rings. The black-and-white tile dance floor was covered with gold glitter.

All that glittered and flowered in the tent was the work of party decorators Robin Rodbell and Nancy Braithwaite.

The chairmen of the ball were Mrs. F. Ross Johnson and Mrs. Erwin Zabin.

Tiffany & Co. and Joseph E. Seagram & Sons were among the evening's benefactors.

Tiffany & Co. provided favors of "Tiffany" perfume and presented maestro Levi and his wife Jacqueline with Tiffany "Tesoro" sport watches as mementos of the tesoro-filled evening.

Atlanta's Affairs to Remember caterers catered with a menu of Asparagus and Smoked Salmon Timbale Prelude set in Topaz Aspic Jewels, Stuffed Veal Roulade with Crabmeat and Fresh Spinach in a Sauce of Mustard Cognac, and a Chocolate Rhapsody Finale of chocolate mousse in a scalloped chocolate shortbread cup topped with whipped cream and fresh strawberries and served on a plate of caramel sauce and chopped nuts.

Dancing followed to the music of no less than the Atlanta Symphony.

Geoffrey Beene/ The First Twenty-Five Years, New York

On September 19, 1988, haute *society of New York along with America's* haute *fashion writers turned out en masse at New York's National Academy of Design to celebrate America's most* haute *couturier, Geoffrey Beene, on his twenty-fifth year as a leading fashion designer.*

After viewing The National Academy's glorious retrospective exhibition of both Beene basics and blockbusters, the 250 well-wishers, scores of them in Geoffrey Beene evening dresses, descended to the Academy's main galleries, both splendid neo-Georgian palace rooms (formerly the reception rooms of scholar, philanthropist and art patron Archer M. Huntington, whose Fifth Avenue house was bequeathed to the Academy in 1940).

The tables of ten were skirted in white with Geoffrey Beene signature black with white polka-dot overcloths. The black ballroom chairs' seats reversed the theme with black dots on a white field.

The incomparably haute *flower arrangements and centerpieces were by New York's most* haute *flower designer Robert Isabell and favored Mr. Beene's favorite color for flowers—white, to the exclusion of all else.*

There were white Casablanca lilies, white hydrangeas, white dahlias, white delphiniums, white scabiosa, white star of Bethlehem lilies, and white tuberoses.

Pots of tuberoses stood about the walls of the main gallery and at the foot of a copy of the Louvre's white marble Venus de Milo, lending their heady perfume to the already heady evening.

The hautely delicious and subtly colored dinner, served on white plates, was catered by Huberts Restaurants and consisted of Shrimp and Smashed Cucumbers, Country Captain Chicken, and two tarts, one of Champagne Grapes, the other of Golden Raspberries. Only the Louis Jadot Fleurie '86 wine was red.

The evening's music was a continuous tape made from selections that have accompanied Mr. Beene's fashion shows over the past twenty-five years.

The gala, a landmark in stylishness, was sponsored by the great New York fashion emporium Bergdorf Goodman, and benefited the National Academy of Design.

Tiffany jewelry designer Paloma Picasso and Mrs. Preston Robert Tisch chaired the evening.

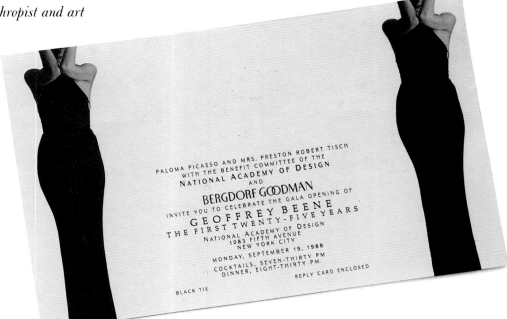

PALOMA PICASSO AND MRS. PRESTON ROBERT TISCH
WITH THE BENEFIT COMMITTEE OF THE
NATIONAL ACADEMY OF DESIGN
AND
BERGDORF GOODMAN
INVITE YOU TO CELEBRATE THE GALA OPENING OF
GEOFFREY BEENE
THE FIRST TWENTY-FIVE YEARS
NATIONAL ACADEMY OF DESIGN
1083 FIFTH AVENUE
NEW YORK CITY
MONDAY, SEPTEMBER 19, 1988
COCKTAILS, SEVEN-THIRTY PM
DINNER, EIGHT-THIRTY PM
REPLY CARD ENCLOSED

BLACK TIE

The Lyric Opera of Chicago Ball

*A*fter the 1988 and thirty-fourth season of the Lyric Opera's opening performance of Vincenzo Bellini's La Sonnambula with Cecilia Gasdia in the role of Amina at Chicago's Civic Opera House, Chicago society, wearing what the Chicago Sun-Times reported as "enough diamonds, emeralds, rubies to pave a block of Michigan Avenue," attended the Opera Ball in the Grand Ballroom of the Chicago Hilton.

Chicago party designer Jason Richards transformed the room's proudly no-holds-barred baroque interior into a shimmering evening sea of blue satin erupting everywhere in geysers of white roses, lilies, gypsophila, and freesia held on American Baroque Revival hotel silver stands.

The tables were skirted in silver lamé and topped with blue satin. The chairs, dressed up with big floppy blue satin bows tied behind their backs, were, as one critic put it, "like Victorian schoolgirls standing for grace before dinner."

Chicagoans glittered in the somnambulist's dream setting as they dined on the menu by Paul G. Demo, the Hilton's director of catering: Mezza Aragosta in Guscio

garnished with asparagus tips, nasturtiums, lemon leaves and pineapple; Lombata di Vitello Arrostita di Funghi; Pasta Tricolore con Pepperoni; Verdura Autunnali and Torta Mascarpone alle Fragole.

Partyers included the William Wood-Princes, Abra and James Wilkin, James and party chairman Ellen O'Connor, Bonnie and John Swearingen, Maria Tallchief Paschen, Chicago Mayor Sawyer; Ambassador Dan and Judith Terra; the Lyric's General Manager Ardis Krainik; Mr. and Mrs. T. Kimball Brooker; and grande dame of dance Ruth Page.

The Michael Carney Orchestra provided dance music.

The Eleanor Naylor Dana Charitable Trust sponsored the La Sonnambula production. Aon Corporation sponsored the opening

night benefit and Texaco Inc. and Merrill Lynch sponsored the Opera Ball, which was presented by the Women's Board of the Lyric Opera (Mrs. T. Kimball Brooker, President).

Alice in Wonderland or A Kid Again, Greenwich

*I*t has oft been stated, in our post-Lewis Carroll world, that if nonsense is not given a role something will be left out. Here at a Greenwich, Connecticut, September 17, 1988, "summer bash," as the host and hostess described it, for three hundred of their friends, a blue-Lurex-clad March Hare presided over the intensely colorful fête design while a bigger than life-sized (whatever that size might be) Humpty-Dumpty held court for "all the king's horses and all the king's men" and any other guests that strayed from the party tent into the brick-walled garden.

Nothing was left out.

The Greenwich Three Hundred arrived at the party site by crossing a bridge over a small stream before coming into the "bottom of the rabbit hole" Carrollian setting. There a carnival entertained them with games and offered a selection of hot dogs, peanuts, popcorn and cotton candy. Guests then proceeded into the tent decorated as a fantasy circus by designer Diana Gould and her associate Dennis Grannan, with

inspirations from an inspired reading of Mother Goose.

They carried out their theme with ribbons of every color streaming from equally colorful gas-filled Mylar balloons; with fantastic, levitating, anthropomorphic beasts glittering in Lurex and costume jewels and crowned with feathers; and with more earthbound centerpieces of late-summer Greenwich flowers.

A hand-painted cutout of an acrobat riding a unicycle moved back and forth on a high wire while juvenilely delinquent and delighted adults perched on Lurex-covered ballroom chairs below.

Thousands of tiny multicolored lights animated the scene.

Stamford, Connecticut's Incredible Edibles caterers' Janet Dresden composed the evening's dinner with Garlic and Parsley Linguini with Shrimp Scampi, Salade Caprese made from sliced beefsteak tomatoes, smoked scamorza cheese, Maui onions, fresh basil and vinaigrette dressing. (The meeting of Capri and Maui surprised no one.) The Incredible Edibles fare continued with Teriyaki-Glazed Salmon Fillets grilled over mesquite, Chateaubriand served with Sauce Béarnaise, Rosemary-roasted Potatoes and Mélange of Summer Grilled Vegetables.

A dessert of Chocolate Pastilles filled with White Chocolate Mousse, Raspberry Mousse and Lemon Mousse

covered with a bittersweet glaze and served in a pool of Crème Anglaise followed.

Then the guests "fell to playing catch-as-catch-can" till the Crème Anglaise "ran out at their heels."

The Splendour in St. Petersburg Ball, Old Westbury

*I*mperial 1988 New York re-created an evening in Imperial Russia on September 24 at the Old Westbury Gardens museum, the stately Charles II-style mansion surrounded by 100 acres of gardens which once upon a time was the residence of Mr. and Mrs. John S. Phipps.

For the Gardens' Splendour in St. Petersburg Ball, whose theme was chosen to recognize the one-thousandth anniversary of Russian Christianity, designer Barry Ferguson of Oyster Bay and New York turned the event's sprawling oval tent into a czarist's dreamworld reminiscent of a stage set for Tschaikovsky's Scheherazade. Tables covered in gold, red and purple paisley, crystal chandeliers, massive silver and gilt candelabra and flamboyant bouquets of red lilies, roses, delphiniums, stems from berry bushes, miniature apples and grapes and a backdrop painted by Ferguson of onion-domed towers all brought a note of bedizened splendor to the Old Westbury, Long Island, gardens.

The dinner, catered by Abigail Kirsch, reflected the late summer

evening's Imperial Russian theme. After a specially created "Balalaika Russe" cocktail mixed from raspberry purée and champagne, the imperial guests—wearing, as the invitation had stipulated, black tie or "court dress" (many of the ladies wore tiaras)—dined imperially on Poached Norwegian Salmon with Dilled Cucumber Salad and Pumpernickel Croustades; Beef Stroganoff with Roasted New Long Island Potatoes and Grilled Red Onions; a Medley of Autumn Vegetables and Strawberries Romanoff, Praline Nuggets and Chocolate Truffles.

Lester Lanin, maestro to the court of Imperial New York for longer than anyone can possibly remember, conducted his much-loved orchestra for dancing from nine to one o'clock.

There were special attractions including the Forbes Fabergé hot-air balloon; a cache of Imperial Russian treasures from the Hillwood Museum, former home of imperial Mrs. Marjorie Merriweather Post, watched over by imperially uniformed guards; a "caviar, blini and champagne feast" table setting by imperial Mrs. William Randolph Hearst, Jr., which included Hearst family Tiffany silver, Baccarat crystal and Russian porcelain; and an imperial floral arrangement by imperial Mrs. Winston F. C. Guest.

In the more sedate dining room of the imperial Phipps family palace,

Prince William Henry of England painted by Thomas Gainsborough and Mrs. Henry Phipps painted by John Singer Sargent looked over a more classically formal dinner setting.

Three generations of the New York imperial Phipps family attended the ball, which was chaired by Mrs. Bronson Trevor, Jr., and vice-chaired by Mrs. John J. Talley.

The ball committee included Mr. and Mrs. Colin Phipps, Mr. and

Mrs. Howard Phipps, Jr., and the even more imperial (if possible) Prince and Princess Alexander Romanoff.

Mr. George D. Phipps was on the Junior Committee.

The Phipps house is on the National Register of Historic Places.

Hispanic Designers' Luncheon for Paloma Picasso, Washington, D.C.

*H*ispanic Designers, Inc., was founded on the premise that the potential for success exists for everyone and that Hispanic Americans are making a positive contribution to American society and should be recognized for their achievements.

At the 1988 Hispanic Designers Gala Benefit under the honorary patronage of First Lady Nancy Reagan, held in Washington, D.C., on September 15, Tiffany jewelry designer Paloma Picasso, who received the year's Moda Award for design excellence, was fêted by a pre-gala showing of her jewelry collection and a luncheon sponsored by Tiffany & Co.

The jeweled event took place at the Willard Intercontinental Hotel's splendid late-Victorian Crystal Room, the site of many of the most elaborate banquets and glittering balls in Washington's history. The room's stately marbleized columns, soaring windows, elaborately carved and paneled walls and ceilings and white-globed Victorian crystal chandeliers echo the bygone era when ten presidents in succession, from Franklin Pierce to Woodrow Wilson, awaited their inaugurations in residence.

Classic Louis XVI chairs surrounded the tables of ten with their white linen cloths and white lace toppers.

Victorian-style floral arrangements of snapdragons, red and lavender roses, alstroemeria and stargazer lilies, freesia, cornflowers, liatris, merry widow tulips, dendrobium orchids and English ivy by Michael Rufino of Rufino Designs were set in neoclassic Tiffany Italian ceramic pots throughout the room.

The Willard staff prepared a luncheon of Chilled Tomato Soup with Fresh Basil Sorbet, Minute of Salmon with an Angel-hair Pasta Timbale and Molded Carrots à la Crème followed by Crème Brûlée with leaf-shaped Almond Wafers Dipped in Chocolate and pale blue frosted Petits Fours tied with frosting ribbons in emulation of Tiffany's signature white-ribboned blue boxes—the kind Paloma Picasso jewels come in.

For the luncheon, Miss Picasso—who once admitted that she "worship(s) style"—wore an Yves Saint Laurent black-and-white jacket with a mid-thigh-length black skirt by Azzedine Alaia, combining two of her favorite fashion designers' work.

Of Hispanic design, Paloma Picasso says, "With Spain it is always a mix of something very extreme and also very restrained—strict and opulent at the same time.

"There is always an element of classicism in everything I do, mixed with an element of fun."

The Union Station Gala, Washington, D.C.

*A*rchitect Daniel H. Burnham, whom Congress chose to design Washington D.C.'s Union Station, had a motto: "Make no small plans." His masterpiece and one of America's premier landmarks was immodestly modeled on the Baths of Diocletian with added inspiration from the Arch of Constantine in Rome.

The train was still king when the titanic transportation palace opened in 1907 complete with Constantinian arches, coffered and vaulted ceilings, majestic skylights and towering Louis Saint-Gaudens statues. However, it would not be many years before air travel would dethrone it as the great gateway to the nation's capital where presidents and their wives greeted kings and queens, as President and Mrs. Franklin D. Roosevelt greeted King George VI and Queen Elizabeth of England on June 8, 1939.

After years of neglect throughout the sixties and seventies, restoration of the station was begun in 1984. Then, on September 28, 1988, at a black-tie gala for twenty-four hundred guests held under the honorary chairmanship of then Vice President and Mrs. Bush and under Union Station's newly gold-leafed vaults glittering in the light of some four thousand candles, its reopening was celebrated at a benefit for the National Trust for Historic Preservation.

Tall five-candle candelabra holding tall red candles tied with colorful orange lily garlands arranged by Vanderbrook Florists were on each of the 240 red, pink and orange chintz-covered tables of ten where celebrants dined on Ridgewell Inc. caterer's dinner of Lobster Quenelles with Sauce Nantua; Twin Fillets of Veal with Tarragon-lime Butter and Beef with Sherry-sautéed Mushrooms; Tomatoes Bienville; a Medley of Vegetables; Corn Rolls and Herbed Pepper Muffins; Watercress, Endive and Pear Salad and Hazelnut Torte Union Station.

Michael Carney and his orchestra provided dance music.

The gala opening's general chairmen were Mr. and Mrs. Robert M. Bass, and the evening's festivities were made possible through a generous grant from the partners of Union Station Venture, Ltd.: LaSalle Partners, Williams Jackson Ewing, and Benjamin Thompson & Associates (the architects for the restoration).

Four months after the gala opening, on January 20, 1989, President Bush celebrated his inauguration at another Union Station Ball. This prototypical palace of the people was back in service much as President Theodore Roosevelt had envisioned it when he signed the act to authorize its construction on February 28, 1903.

Paige Rense's New York Winter Antiques Show Dinner

*E*ditor-in-Chief of Architectural Digest *and ex-officio United States "Secretary of Interiors" Paige Rense annually celebrates the opening of New York's prestigious Winter Antiques Show with a dinner for interior designers, writers and just good friends who more than annually contribute to her prestigious publication.*

The January 20, 1989, Inauguration Day dinner given in the Versailles Room at the Carlyle Hotel successfully vied with inaugural events being given in Washington, D.C., the same evening.

Paige Rense loyalists who dined on Quennelles en Brochette with Sauce Nantua, Rack of Lamb Persillé and Crème Brulée with Fresh Berries included Marietta Tree, Susan Mary Alsop, National Academy of Design director John Dobkin, pianists and writers Arthur Gold and Arthur Fizdale, designer and Winter Antiques Show impresario Mario Buatta, fellow designers Jay Spectre, Mary Meehan, Robert Metzger, Juan Pablo Molyneux, and Jean-François

Daigre, antique pasha Bernard Steinitz, photographer Feliciano, socialite and public relations ace Marilyn Evins, telejournalist Elsa Klensch, and sixty-five others.

Ex-officio United States "Secretary of Horticulture" and party prestidigitator Marlo Phillips "breaking away" she said, "from the monotony of round tables and chairs," sent fifty vintage-fabric-wrapped bowls of densely packed flowers zigzagging down the center of a single long table for eighty.

"Marlo" said Aileen Mehle in the New York Post's "Suzy" column, "had gone fabulously wild creating a tableau of intriguing art objects from the Newell Art Galleries, including beautiful little antique children's chairs running up and down the table, interspersed with towering candelabra with colored tapers and a garden's worth of the most beautiful flowers, from simple little white daisies to exotic orchids pushed in all manner of vases, pots and containers."

The Tiffany Wedding *Dinner, New York*

*I*n L'Orangerie of the New York Mayfair Regent Hotel's Le Cirque restaurant, long-favored family dining room of Manhattan society, Mrs. Seymour Berkson (more publicly known as columnist and fashion world publicist legend Eleanor Lambert), Mrs. John R. Drexel III of Newport and New York and Mrs. Elton M. Hyder, Jr., of Fort Worth and the music world hosted a small formal dinner for

Mrs. Seymour Berkson
Mrs. John R. Drexel, III
Mrs. Elton M. Hyder, Jr.
request the pleasure of your company
at a dinner in honor of
John Loring
to celebrate the publication of
The Tiffany Wedding
Tuesday, the fourth of October
at eight o'clock
L'Orangerie of Le Cirque
The Mayfair Regent Hotel

R.S.V.P.
Mrs. Eckardt
(212) 605-4125   Black tie

seventy friends to celebrate the 1988 publication of John Loring's fourth book, The Tiffany Wedding.

The early autumn event was decorated by Manhattan party design legend John Funt in red, purple, gold and white with dramatic pink-gel spotlighting.

The seven red-clothed tables of ten had centerpieces combining boldly scaled crystal vases, urns and candlesticks—all designed by Loring for Tiffany's—holding arrangements of fleshy purple and white orchids accented with gold-sprayed pears, walnuts and miniature pumpkins.

Le Cirque's patrón, Sirio Maccioni, personally selected the northern Italian autumn menu of Crêpes d'Homard, Navarin d'Agneau, two soufflés, Italian wines and champagne.

Satirical songster Christopher Mason sang a song about everything from John Loring's Arizona ranch childhood to Tiffany silver, all to the amusement of almost everyone including Estée Lauder, Mr. and Mrs. Paul Hallingby, Mr. and Mrs. Louis Auchincloss, Carolina and Renaldo Herrera, Ambassador Selwa Roosevelt, Mr. and Mrs. William Chaney, Mr. and Mrs. Nicholas Drexel, Joanne Toors Cummings, Aileen "Suzy" Mehle, Jerome Zipkin, Isabelle "Ultra Violet" Dufresne, Marisol, Pauline Trigère, Mary McFadden, Jean Tailer, Lee Thaw, Arnold Scaasi, Patrick McCarthy, Carrie Donovan, Jane Lane and other habitués of L'Orangerie.

There was a copy of The Tiffany Wedding in a Tiffany blue box for everyone.

The Chicago Opera Theater Gala

Chicago's Drake is one of the few hotels on the National Register of Historic Places. Its popular banquet rooms, the Gold Coast Room, the Ballroom, and the French Room, much loved by Chicagoans, have hosted the antics of Chicago society since the hotel's New Year's Eve opening celebration on December 31, 1920.

For the Chicago Opera Theater's 1988 gala fund-raiser on October 21, Chicago gala designer Jason Richards brought proper operatic sparkle to the Drake Hotel's historic Gold Coast Room, draping the handsome room's tables in black, gold and silver-striped cloths from Carousel Linens Boutique. Richards's centerpieces were small Post-Modernist gazebos with brass foundation platforms and arches separated by Lucite columns and crowned by lofty bouquets of all-white tulips, lilies and freesias mixed with ferns. Black napkins tied with white bows sat on white plates.

Sitting among the Gold Coast's towering colonnades with their spiraling gilt plasterwork vines reflected in the polished Tennessee marble dance floor, the four hundred Opera Theater supporters dined on a banquet provided by the Drake Hotel's catering specialists, who have in their time produced banquets for Queen Elizabeth II of England and the late Emperor Hirohito of Japan, as well as Wild West buffets and Bavarian feasts for lesser visitors to the shores of Lake Michigan.

Swiss-born executive chef Leo Waldmeier's menu included Mixed Seafood served with Oriental Salad and Curry Sauce; Petit Filet of Beef with Marrow Crust and Cabernet Sauvignon Sauce; Pommes Savoyard and Snowpeas with Toasted Pine Nuts; followed by Chocolate Truffle with a Pear Fan and Grand Marnier sauce.

The highlight of the evening was a postprandial march to the tune of "The Night They Invented Champagne" of forty Drake waiters bearing silver trays of Tiffany blue boxes containing two Tiffany champagne flutes for each guest.

Mr. Wallace Steiner and Mrs. Howard Zodikoff chaired the event.

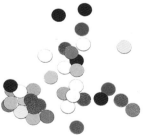

The Brooklyn Academy of Music's Gala of Stars

*T*o launch the Brooklyn Academy of Music's 1988 Next Wave Festival on October 19, Philip Morris Companies Inc. sponsored a benefit dinner preceded by a special one-hour performance from Bob Telson and Lee Breuer's music-theater pageant The Warrior Ant.

Bianca Jagger, Gala chairwoman, chose a tropical décor by tropical-and-other-themes party design ace Robert Isabell to complement the Afro-Caribbean music, Japanese puppetry and African storytelling of The Warrior Ant.

On the Academy's grand stage, since its 1908 opening frequented by stars such as Enrico Caruso, Isadora Duncan, Arturo Toscanini, Anna Pavlova, Gustav Mahler, Sergei Rachmaninoff, Ellen Terry and Mary Pickford, Isabell secured 5-foot-tall banana trees to his hot-pink-covered tabletops and decorated the banana trees and the Academy's chandeliers with huge crêpe-paper flowers in vibrant colors.

The food for the evening, served on black porcelain plates, was prepared

by Tentation Catering to carry out The Warrior Ant tropical theme. There was a Wild Mushroom Flan followed by Salmon with Sorrel Butter Sauce served with Wild Rice, and a dessert of Passion Fruit, Mango and Lime Mousse topped with Fresh Fruit and Raspberry Sauce.

Following dinner, two reggae bands, Souljah's and Morgan's Heritage, played for the Gala of Stars guests, including stars Lauren Hutton, Paul Schrader, Bianca Jagger, Harvey Keitel, Mary Beth Hurt, Jim Henson, Spalding Gray, Mitch Miller, Michael Graves and Dick Cavett.

Opening Night Committee stars included: Anne Bass; Candice Bergen and Louis Malle; David Bowie; Tina Brown; H.S.H. Princess Caroline of Monaco; Glenn Close; Richard Gere; Whoopi Goldberg; Patricia Kennedy Lawford; Norman Mailer and Brooke Shields.

The 1988 Royal Chase Committee Luncheon, Nashville

*T*o honor the "Royal Box Holders" at the October 14th "One Million Dollar Sport of Kings Challenge" steeplechase held at Nashville's Warner Park Steeplechase Course, the Royal Chase committee held a pre-race luncheon for 350, followed by a post-race tea for 675 in the presence of H.R.H. the Princess Royal (more popularly known as Princess Anne).

The luncheon, held under an expansive tent provided by Arrow Special Events Co. of Richmond, Virginia, was decorated by Mrs. W. Alexander Steele III and Mrs. Hunter Armistead after a creative design by Mrs. Henry F. Lochte with black-and-white-striped toppers on marigold-yellow tablecloths. Black lacquered baskets with Royal Chase crests held breadsticks for centerpieces, and wild field flowers were tucked into the luncheon napkins and tied with marigold-yellow bows.

The Princess Royal's box had a more elaborate centerpiece of marigolds, pheasant feathers, lilies and pepper berries arranged in a black classical garden urn, and the chairs in the royal box had black-and-white-striped covers.

Racing enthusiasts lunched on Tennessee Caviar Pie, Braided Salmon with Tarragon Sauce and Toasted Pine Nuts, Spinach Timbale with Lingonberry Sauce, chilled Tortellini with Country Vegetables Julienne and assorted Chocolate Truffles prepared by Nashville Hyatt Regency executive chef Jim Higgins.

The post-race tea took place in the Royal Enclosure, an adjoining tent decorated by Sandra Steele and Mikel Lovvorn with towering arrangements of autumn leaves, pheasant feathers, Indian corn, and pepper berry trees inhabited by stuffed birds from the Tennessee Wildlife Association.

The Princess Royal rode in and won the second race on Wood Chisel, owned by Nashvillager Jerry Carroll, giving the afternoon an infusion of surprise and heartfelt excitement.

Tiffany's contributed an appropriately large and elaborate sterling silver Tiffany-designed-and-made cup to serve as a perpetual trophy, given each year to the winner of the international, four-race "One Million Dollar Sport of Kings Challenge" series.

The event was chaired by Mrs. Henry W. Hooker and Mrs. Sidney S. McAlister.

Proceeds went to the Princess Royal's favorite charity, Save the Children, and to the preservation and educational programs of Travellers' Rest Historic House Museum.

The Stop Cancer Gala at the Winter Garden, New York

Beneath a spotlit grove of 45-foot California palms which were in turn growing beneath the 120-foot-high unlit glass ceiling of New York's World Financial Center's Winter Garden, eight hundred supporters of billionaire philanthropist Dr. Armand Hammer of Occidental Petroleum's "Stop Cancer" foundation paid $2,500 each to sit at the pink-toned tables of the Stop Cancer kickoff dinner that raised an astounding two million dollars toward Dr. Hammer's goal of one billion dollars.

Co-chairing the October 12, 1988, gala along with Dr. and Mrs. Hammer were Mr. and Mrs. John W. Kluge and Mr. and Mrs. Albert Reichmann, who underwrote the entire evening and whose firm, Olympia & York, built the Winter Garden—"perhaps the grandest public space built in New York since Grand Central Terminal," according to Paul Goldberger, Architecture Editor of the New York Times.

The evening began with a concert by the Philadelphia Orchestra conducted by Mstislav Rostropovich and with Isaac Stern playing the violin. That was followed by jazz pianist Marian McPartland's reception recital before dinner.

Capricho Inc. caterers prepared a relatively (as these things go) simple dinner of Saumon en Croûte à la Florentine; Medallion de Veau Sauté au Vin et Champignons; Meringue Flambé aux Fraises Sauce Sabayon and Chocolate Truffles.

The refreshingly unstudied all red and pink rose and dahlia-packed flower arrangements were by highly imaginative Manhattan florist Twigs with table décor by Wendy Goidell Flowers.

Silver-foil "crackers" at each place held a 1-ounce silver ingot signed by World Financial Center architect Cesar Pelli. The ingots commemorated this gala opening of the center, attended by, among others, New York Governor Cuomo, Mayor Koch, the Rupert Murdochs, the Randolph Hearsts, the Arthur Krims, the Louis Nizers, Steve Ross, Rhonda (Fleming) and Ted Mann, Beverly Sills, Barbara Walters, Abigail Van Buren, the Robert Campeaus, James Wolfensohn and Helen Boehm.

Merv Griffin acted as master of ceremonies.

President Reagan and ex-Presidents Nixon and Carter all sent messages.

The Coconuts' New Year's Eve, Palm Beach

For over forty years American society's most partying bachelors, joining forces under the banner of "The Coconuts Club," have held what by many in the know is rated as the only New Year's Eve party to be invited to in America.

Palm Beach is always the setting, and the 1988 Coconuts' party was fittingly held at that grand old aristocrat of resort hotels, The Breakers.

The Coconuts' longest-standing member, though no-longer bachelor, the Honorable Guilford Dudley, Jr., co-chaired the event with his glamorous and tirelessly party-chairing wife Jane, who when she is not chairing benefit galas finds time to sit on Tiffany & Co.'s board of directors.

The Coconuts' 246 guests danced in the New Year to the music of the Neil Smith Orchestra in a witty devil-may-care-we-plan-to-enjoy-ourselves décor by Palm Beach Display complete with electric palm trees, paper hats, noisemakers and balloons.

There to have high fun, high society felt no obligation to dine on a 1988 social season haute cuisine

menu of salmon with sauce, veal with more sauce and designer vegetables followed by a chocolate dessert bathed in "coulis de framboise."

They reveled instead in traditional American Turkey Hash, Scrambled Eggs, Bacon and Sausage, Pancakes,

French Toast, Maple Syrup, Honey, Jams and Jellies and Fresh Fruit, all washed down with plenty of champagne while the Villa Medici-inspired twin belvedere towers of the ever-dignified pleasure palace, The Breakers, looked on in complete approval.

The Literary Lions Dinner, New York

*T*o honor literary friends of its research libraries and raise moneys for its General Book Fund, the New York Public Library has for eight years held a "Literary Lions" dinner.

The 1988 dinner, held on November 10, was, like its seven predecessors, decorated by designer Peggy Mulholland. In the pine-paneled Arents Reading Room, of the Arents Tobacco Collection under the watchful eye of "Squanto" the collection's cigar-store Indian, Mulholland covered the tables with red tapestry and tied cream damask napkins with red silk cords, using antique gilded lion's head scarf clasps in lieu of napkin rings. Her thematic centerpieces were Venetian-style garden lions wearing reading glasses sitting in beds of ivy and white orchids.

The twenty-six "Lions"— including Art Buchwald, Peter Gay, Barbara Goldsmith, Alfred Kazin, Stanley Kunitz, R.W.B. Lewis, Jessica Mitford, Herbert Mitgang, Gloria Naylor, Emily Prager, Leo Steinberg and August Wilson, and their well-read and well-heeled admirers, including Brooke Astor,

Henry and Nancy Kissinger, Jacqueline Onassis, Louis Auchincloss, Lily Auchincloss, Enid Haupt, Patricia Mosbacher, Dr. and Mrs. Vartan Gregorian, Bill Blass, Sid Bass and Mercedes Kellogg, Annette Reed, Jayne Wrightsman, John and Susan Gutfreund, Lord Weidenfeld, and Henry Kravis and Carolyne Roehm—dined on a gloriously sensible Glorious Foods meal of Lentil Soup with Country Sausage; Roast Fillet of Lamb with Basil Sauce; and Caramelized Rice Pudding with Coconut Ice Cream.

Mortimer Zuckerman was honorary chairman and underwriter of the evening, which was chaired by Lily Auchincloss.

After dinner, Christopher Plummer gave a tour de force reading of two excerpts from works by Stephen Leacock in the Library's Trustees' Room.

The Reagans' Final State Dinner, Washington, D.C.

*T*he State Dining Room of the White House retains the oak wall paneling, Corinthian pilasters, lighting fixtures and delicately carved frieze of its 1902 renovation by architects McKim, Mead & White completed during Theodore Roosevelt's presidency, and since 1902 changes in décor have been few. However, the large moose head hung by Roosevelt over the fireplace has long since been replaced by George Healy's contemplative portrait of Abraham Lincoln painted in 1869 and bequeathed to the White House in 1939 by Lincoln's daughter-in-law; the oak paneling has been painted over, first in celadon green by the Trumans in 1952 and then in antique ivory by the Kennedys in 1962; the Reagans added the gold silk damask curtains and elaborate valances in 1981.

Here on November 16, 1988, the President and Mrs. Reagan hosted the final state dinner of the Reagan Era, honoring the Prime Minister of Great Britain and Northern Ireland, Margaret Thatcher, and Mr. Thatcher, and so closed a brilliant chapter in the history of American parties.

The State Dining Room was in full dress for the occasion in peach tablecloths with peach overlays and white damask napkins with the presidential seal. The settings included vermeil flatware, Morgantown crystal and the Reagan red-and-gold Lenox china.

Topiary trees of peach roses designed by "court florist" Nancy Clark decorated the tables as well as the three console tables with gilt eagle supports by A. H. Davenport Co. of Boston installed by McKim, Mead & White in 1902.

The legendarily superb White House chefs that evening prepared a gala menu of Baby Lobster Bellevue, Caviar Yogurt Sauce, Curried Croissant; Roasted Saddle of Veal Périgourdine, Jardinière of Vegetables, Asparagus with Hazelnut Butter; Autumn Mixed Salad, Selection of Cheese; Chestnut Marquise, Pistachio Sauce, Orange Tuiles and Ginger Twigs. The wines were: Saintsbury Chardonnay Reserve 1987; Stag's Leap Wine Cellars Cabernet Sauvignon 1978; Schramsberg Crémant Demi Sec 1984.

During dinner, the U.S. Marine Orchestra provided music from the Grand Foyer. The U.S. Army Strolling Strings played in the State Dining Room during the dessert course, and the U.S. Marine Dance

Band provided music for dancing in the Grand Foyer following an after-dinner performance by pianist Michael Feinstein in the East Room.

Football great Roosevelt Grier, who was among the guests, commented that Reagan had brought "a great amount of elegance and style to the country." Fellow guest, writer Tom Bonfire of the Vanities Wolfe, added that the Reagan years would be remembered "for the sense of optimism he brought to the country."

The evening was in any case, as Margaret Thatcher put it, "a very special occasion."

The cast of the closing-night performance included then Vice President and Mrs. Bush, Secretary of State and Mrs. Shultz, British Ambassador Sir Anthony Ackland and Lady Ackland, Chief Justice and Mrs. Rehnquist, Senator and Mrs. Hatfield, Mr. and Mrs. Walter Annenberg, Malcolm Forbes, Mikhail Baryshnikov, Evangeline Bruce, David Hockney, Mrs. Robert "Oatsie" Charles, U.S. Ambassador to Great Britain and Mrs. Price, The Reverend and Mrs. Billy Graham, Beverly Sills, Mr. and Mrs. Henry Kissinger, Mrs. Bob Hope, Joseph Brodsky, Chief of Protocol Selwa Roosevelt and Archibald B. Roosevelt, Jr., Tom Selleck, Andrew Lloyd Webber, Mr. and Mrs. Caspar W. Weinberger and Loretta Young.

State Department Dinner in Honor of Secretary of State and Mrs. George P. Shultz, Washington, D.C.

*T*he Friends of Art Preservation in Embassies was established in October 1986 to assist the U.S. Department of State in exhibiting and preserving American fine art and furnishings in one hundred and twenty U.S. embassies abroad.

In a farewell salute to President and Mrs. Ronald Reagan, the organization held a reception on November 29, 1988, at the White House. The reception was followed by a dinner in honor of Secretary of State and Mrs. George P. Shultz in the Benjamin Franklin Diplomatic Reception Room of the U.S. Department of State.

In step with the regal décor of the reception hall with its imposing fluted red marble columns topped by gilded Corinthian capitals and its six dazzling crystal chandeliers, "court party designer" John Funt aided by Mrs. Lee Kimche McGrath, Director of the Art in Embassies Program, covered tables and ballroom chair cushions in bright canary yellow silk moiré and mixed yellow and red tulips and roses in Tiffany Private Stock porcelain soup tureens as centerpieces for the dinner.

The State Department chefs offered a simple and stylish palace dinner of Ragout of Seafood, Rosemary-grilled Poussin, and Chestnut Semifreddo.

Tiffany & Co. offered the party favors at each place wrapped in traditional Tiffany blue boxes.

The Friends of Art Preservation in Embassies is chaired by the Honorable Leonore Annenberg, former Chief of Protocol. Mrs. William H. (Wendy) Luers is president, and the Honorable Daniel J. Terra, U.S. Ambassador-at-Large for Cultural Affairs, is honorary chairman.

Mr. and Mrs. David Paul's Six Chefs Dinner, La Gorce Island

*I*n January 1988 at a charity auction in Paris to benefit Very Special Arts, part of the Kennedy Foundation for handicapped children, chairman of Miami's Centrust Savings Bank David Paul and his beautiful young wife Sandra placed the winning bid of $30,000 on the services of France's six greatest chefs to cook a dinner anywhere in the world.

The Pauls and fifty-eight friends enjoyed their winnings on December 3rd, 4,715 miles from Paris at the Paul compound on La Gorce Island just offshore from Miami. In a 40-foot white tent lavishly decorated for the evening by designer and past master of floral still life James Goslee with embroidered tablecloths, leaf-shaded candles and

Chef	Restaurant
Paul Bocuse	Paul Bocuse
Pierre Troisgros	Trois Gros
Michel Rostang	Michel Rostang
Jacques Maximin	Le Doyen
Gaston Lenôtre	Le Pré Catelan
Michel Lorain	La Côte Saint-Jacques

breathtakingly beautiful centerpieces conjured from every imaginable sort of delicate flower mixed with fruits, aromatic herbs and vegetables, the Pauls' and their guests reveled in the definitive 1980s dinner.

The first course, Paul Bocuse's Soupe de Truffes Noires, made with beef stock, microspecks of chicken, fois gras, carrots, mushrooms and shallots baked in a Limoges porcelain soup bowl especially inscribed for the occasion and sealed with puff pastry. The wine was Montée-de-Tonnerre Chablis 1981.

The second course, billed as "Les Petits Oeufs de Caille en Coque d'Oursin" was replaced by Michel Rostang with an improvised dish of Beluga Caviar in a nest of Angel-hair Pasta served on a bed of onions with a reduced cream sauce. (The sea urchins scheduled to be flown in from Maine had not arrived.) The wine was Domaine Leflaive Puligny-Montrachet Les Pucelles 1983.

The third course, Jacques Maximin's Loup de Mer à la Croûte de Legumes, sea bass baked in a "crust" of mousse of carrots, spinach and zucchini served with a fennel-scented Béarnaise sauce that Maximin said had been whipped for one hour and ten minutes. More Montrachet accompanied the bass.

The fourth course, Michel Lorain's Foie Gras Poêle aux Olives—New York foie gras poached in duck stock and flavored with ripe black olives.

The wine was Robert Mondavi Opus One 1983.

The fifth course, Pierre Troisgros's Filet de Canard aux Divers Poivres à la Gastrique de Fruits Rouges—duck breast in a reduced sauce of raspberries, strawberries and currants flavored with ginger and both green and black peppercorns. More Opus One accompanied the duck.

And finally for dessert, Gaston Lenôtre's Pré Catalan cake, a vanilla-flavored white cake topped with chocolate mousse and crème anglaise. The wine was Dom Pérignon rosé en magnum 1980.

Sandra Paul, quietly dressed in a black-and-white gown by Bill Blass, summed up the feelings of hostesses and chairladies at the ends of gala dinners. "As for the hostess," she said, "it's all absolutely wonderful, if her dinner partner is absolutely charming."

Mrs. Paul

Menu

La Soupe de Truffes Noires V.G.E.
Les Petits Oeufs de Caille en
Coque d'Oursin
Le Loup à la Croûte de Légumes
Le Foie Gras Poêlé aux Olives
Le Filet de Canard aux Divers
Poivres à la Gastrique de
Fruits Rouges
Le Pré Catelan

Puligny Montrachet 1953
Opus One 1984 Robert Mondavi
Dom Pérignon rosé en magnum 1980
de Moët & Chandon
Cordials

Le 3 décembre 1988

The Metropolitan Museum of Art's Costume Institute Gala, New York

For years the Costume Institute's early December party at the Metropolitan Museum has been the quintessential New York social/media event of the social/media season.

The 1988 extravaganza, held on December fifth to fête the opening of the Institute's "From Queen to Empress: Victorian Dress 1837–1877," brought out all Imperial New York's fashion and social royalty, who were rated forty-eight hours later by Women's Wear Daily *according to their costumes as "Queen Mother, Princesses, Duchesses, Prince, Little Kings, Damsels in Distress and Commoners."*

Imperial party designer and long-standing official Costume Institute gala designer John Funt transformed the Met's restaurant into a Crystal Palace-scaled winter garden complete with a white marble Victorian lady in a grotto of moss and ferns, potted palms everywhere, and tables and chairs covered in a red paisley by Quadrille for Bloomcraft.

Glorious Foods created·an imperial and very sensibly English dinner of Prawns and Crab Claws with Cocktail and Rémoulade Sauces, Crown Roast of Lamb with Chestnut Stuffing, and Victorian Pudding Flambé with Raisin Cinnamon Custard Sauce and Stewed Figs.

Long-standing imperial Costume Institute Gala chairman Mrs. William F. Buckley, Jr., was chairman.

The "Party Palace" Met's imperial floral designer Chris Giftos did an 8-by-10-foot Victorian centerpiece to greet guests at the museum's entrance.

Imperial guests included "Queen Mother" Estée Lauder; "Little Kings" Henry Kravis and Henry Kissinger; "Prince" John F. Kennedy, Jr.; "Princesses" Laura Tisch and Susan Burden; "Duchesses" Nan Kempner, Anne Bass, Georgette Mosbacher and Lynn Wyatt; "Mistress of the Household" Ivana Trump; "Lord Big Bucks" John and Laura Pomerantz, who underwrote the "From Queen to Empress" exhibition; "The Dowager" Drue Heinz; and plenty of "Commoners" who preferred not to be counted.

Mrs. Albert Lasker's Annual December Dinner, New York

*T*aking time out once each year from her fund-raising in support of medical research, Mrs. Albert Lasker gives a dinner for her one hundred-plus closest friends at that mecca of gastronomy and flowers, New York's La Grenouille. No party of New York's December social season is more enjoyed or more sparkling or more prestigious.

Charles Masson, son of La Grenouille's founder and a wizard of floral decoration, filled the restaurant with flowers in Mrs. Lasker's favorite shades of pink

which range from just off white to just about red—"Omega," "Greta" and "Kryllemi" roses mixed with tulips and branches of quince flown in one week before from the French Riviera to be perfect for the occasion.

The Grenouille's chef Gérard Chotard and sous-chef Jean-Claude Parachini prepared L'aspic de Fois Gras aux Truffes, Filets de Sole Farcis en Crème de Homard, Sal Picon (diced baby artichokes with lobster and mushrooms, port and tarragon), White Basmati Rice with Truffles, a Bombe Glacée, and Petits Fours.

The legendary Lester Lanin and his orchestra played dance music, and the small silk-shaded gilt bronze lamps on La Grenouille's tables illuminated one hundred contented friends of the legendary Mary Lasker.

Diner de Noël

L'Aspic de Foie Gras aux Truffes
Les Filets de Sole Farcis
en Crème de Homard
La Bombe Gala
Café
Petits Fours

CHÂTEAU LAFAURIE-PEYRAGUEY 1985
CHÂTEAU FUISSÉ 1986
TAITTINGER LA FRANÇAISE EN MAGNUMS

Lundi, 12 Décembre, 1988

Katharine Johnson's Dinner, New York

*I*ntricately layered and textured beyond imagination, opulent beyond reason, luxurious beyond description, the objet d'art-infested floral extravaganzas of New York's floral sorceress-in-residence Marlo Phillips bring delight, exhilaration and just plain joy into society's celebrations.

Here for a festive December 1, 1988, dinner at the Manhattan home of Mrs. Katharine Johnson, Marlo's rich concoctions of apricot roses, purple and white cattleya orchids, blue hydrangeas, red anemones, peach carnations, and morella were surrounded by capriciously whimsical arrangements of multicolored candles held by polychromed bronze Moors, and a variety of more traditional candlesticks.

The floral-print-covered tables were set with mismatched porcelain crystal and silver including Tiffany's Private Stock "Cirque Chinois" hand-painted porcelain and "Shell and Thread" sterling silver flatware.

Above the sideboard, which boasted a trio of Marlo fruit and artichoke and flower compositions, a painting

of a bedizened moorish warrior took the splendid setting in stride.

Mrs. Johnson's guests each received a copy of the book The Language of Flowers wrapped and decorated by Marlo with fans and masks and bits of lace and ribbon.

Classic white damask napkins were essential, Marlo felt, to anchor

this ultimate setting for a smaller private party.

The menu featured Pudding de Homard, Lapin à la Solognote, Subric d'épinard, Subric de Marrons, Salade de Mâche et Betterave, Omelette Norvégienne aux trois parfums, vanille, chocolat, café, Petits Gâteaux.

Spirit of the City Award Dinner, New York

*F*or this early December Spirit of the City Award Dinner held in the majestic Synod Hall adjoining New York's Cathedral of St. John the Divine, master of floral design Preston Bailey decked the hall's candle-lit chandeliers with hundreds of yards of gold tulle and imaginatively decorated the outer walls with massive gilt frames enclosing floral still lifes in the style of seventeenth-century Dutch masters. In each still life, Tiffany hand-painted French faience vases held mixtures of snapdragons, lilies, tulips, eucalyptus berries and heather.

Bailey's tables were covered in moss green taffeta with 4-to-7-foot-tall hand-forged iron candlesticks and centerpiece baskets packed with dried and fresh flowers—hydrangeas, orchids, roses, celosia, heather and tulips.

Glorious Foods served a dinner of Marinated Scallops, Roast Veal Larded with Ham, and Apple Brown Betty with Vanilla Ice Cream.

Mrs. Saul Steinberg and Mr. Christopher Forbes chaired the evening.

Awards went to Mrs. Douglas MacArthur, the New York Public

Library's Vartan Gregorian, and to Aileen Mehle, the New York Post columnist "Suzy" who noted in her column "The Cathedral wants us to know that these prestigious awards are presented annually to individuals whose personal endeavors identify with the mission of St. John the Divine—'to make New York a better place to live'."

Proceeds from the evening funded the Cathedral's charitable programs.

The Baron and Baroness di Portanova's Christmas Party, Houston

*F*or no-holds-barred glamour, no party of the 1988 Christmas season could top the Baron and Baroness di Portanova's dinner dance for 120 friends held on Tuesday the 20th at their mansion in Houston's River Oaks.

The di Partanovas' vast entertainment area, a glassed-over garden which Houston Chronicle columnist Betty Ewing described as "vaguely comparable in size to a regulation football field plus end zones with an Olympic-sized blue-water pool in the center" was, Ewing noted, "like an MGM movie set of the good old days."

Designer Don Bolin, who goes as "Houston's Michelangelo of the fancy party circuit," floated life-sized illuminated mannequin angels over gold lamé-covered tables of ten, each named for a Christmas carol. "Illusion is the thing," said Bolin. "It's the theater, it's the circus, it's spiritual, it's fun," said famed eye specialist Dr. Louis Girard.

"Tout Texas" was there: Lynn and Oscar Wyatt; Joanne and Lloyd Davis; Dallas philanthropist Nancy Hamon; Lupe Murchison; Dorothy Heyser; Virginia Murchison Linthicum; Dallas oilman Bill Lee; best-selling writer Nancy Holmes; and others too Texan to mention.

The choir of the Good Hope Missionary Baptist Church on North MacGregor Way sang; and, after a dinner of Smoked Salmon Surprise, French Hen Stuffed with Wild Rice and Foie Gras followed by a fabulously rich Fruit Compote, the di Portanovas' guests danced to the Mark Northan Ensemble's music and admired Don Bolin's 30-foot Christmas tree in front of the di Portanova guesthouse across the pool.

The "di Portanova party was a jewel, even in Tiffany's eyes," was Betty Ewing's headline in the Houston Chronicle. It was the prototypical big American party—illusion, theater, movie set, circus, whimsy, fun.

Photography Credits

Pages 18 and 19—Ralph Morse, *Life* Magazine. © 1957 by Time Inc.

New York Public Library Ten Treasures Dinner—Jesse Gerstein

Irving Berlin's 100th Birthday—Peter Vitale

The New York Philharmonic Ball—Jesse Gerstein

An Evening with Calvin Klein to Benefit the Ellington Fund—Jesse Gerstein

The Nelson A. Rockefeller Public Service Award Dinner—Jesse Gerstein

Mrs. John Kluge's Birthday Party—Jesse Gerstein

The Opening of the New York Central Park Zoo—Jesse Gerstein

Ambassador and Countess Wachtmeister's Dinner—Jesse Gerstein

Mrs. Virginia S. Milner's Hawaiian Luau Honoring Mr. and Mrs. Walter Annenberg—Steven Rothfeld

Mrs. Lawrence Copley Thaw's Dinner in Honor of Mrs. Guilford Dudley, Jr.—Billy Cunningham

Mr. and Mrs. Milton Petrie's Fourth of July Party—Jesse Gerstein

Walter Gubelmann's Eightieth Birthday Party—Jesse Gerstein

The Tiffany Feather Ball—Billy Cunningham and Jesse Gerstein

The Swan Ball—Jesse Gerstein

The Southampton Hospital Ball—Jesse Gerstein

Blair House Tea Reception—Jesse Gerstein

Lintas Worldwide Reception—Jesse Gerstein

Green Animals Children's Picnic—Curtice Taylor

The Parrish Art Museum Dance—Curtice Taylor

Bernstein at Seventy—Jesse Gerstein

Snowmass Picnic—Steven Rothfeld

Cocktails Aboard the *Trump Princess*—Billy Cunningham

The Atlanta Symphony Ball—Jesse Gerstein

Geoffrey Beene/The First Twenty-Five Years—Curtice Taylor

The Lyric Opera of Chicago Ball—Billy Cunningham

Alice in Wonderland or A Kid Again—Curtice Taylor

The Splendour in St. Petersburg Ball—Bill Wright

Hispanic Designers' Luncheon for Paloma Picasso—Jesse Gerstein

Paige Rense's New York Winter Antiques Show Dinner—Billy Cunningham

The Tiffany Wedding Dinner—Billy Cunningham

The Union Station Gala—Curtice Taylor

The Chicago Opera Theater Gala—Jesse Gerstein

The Brooklyn Academy of Music's Gala of Stars—Billy Cunningham

The 1988 Royal Chase Committee Luncheon—Billy Cunningham

The Stop Cancer Gala at the Winter Garden—Jesse Gerstein

The Coconuts' New Year's Eve—Billy Cunningham

The Literary Lions Dinner—Billy Cunningham

The Reagans' Final State Dinner—Jesse Gerstein

State Department Dinner in Honor of Secretary of State and Mrs. George P. Shultz—Billy Cunningham

Mr. and Mrs. David Paul's Six Chefs Dinner—Billy Cunningham

The Metropolitan Museum of Art's Costume Institute Gala—Billy Cunningham

Mrs. Albert Lasker's Annual December Dinner—Billy Cunningham

Katharine Johnson's Dinner—Curtice Taylor

Spirit of the City Award Dinner—Jesse Gerstein

The Baron and Baroness di Portanova's Christmas Party—Billy Cunningham

...s of the
...Designers Gala
...any & Co.
...dially invites you to
...a luncheon
and
...rivate viewing of
Paloma Picasso Jewelry Collection
...ay, the fifteenth of September
...seven-thirty o'clock
...in the
...tal Room

Mrs. Vincent Astor, Honorary Chairm...
Annette Reed, Honorary Chairman
Mrs. Donald Newhouse, General Chairm...
of
The Ten Treasures Dinner
and the Trustees of
T' New York Public Library
...l t...nd dinner on

The Women's Committee of
The New York Zoological Society
requests the pleasure of your company
...t a dinner dance
to celebrate the opening of
The New Central Park Zoo
on Tues...y, the twenty-first of June
at seven o'clock

at the ...
at Batt...
New Yor...
October 12, 198...
...day, October 1...
...Card

The pleasure of your company
is requested at
Bal Masque VIII
"A Mystical Evening"
celebrating Chicago Opera Theater's
Fifteenth Anniversary
Friday, October 21, 1988
at seven o'clock
The Drake
Gold C...

Taittinger C'...

ASCAP and Carnegie Hall
present
A Gala Evening
celebrating
IRVING BERLIN'S 100th BIRTHDAY

Among those appearing on stage:

Leonard Bernstein
Willie Nelson
Frank Sinatra
Isaac Stern
Additional Guest Artists to be ann...

Wednesday, May the ele...
Nineteen hundred and e...
7:30 p.m.